THE
GREAT BARRIER REEF
Dive Guide

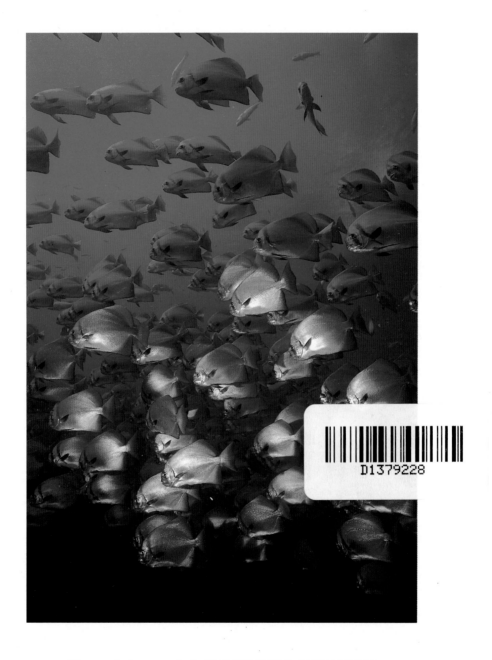

Text and photographs by ROBERTO RINALDI

Editing provided by Diving Science and Technology Corp. (DSAT)
a corporate affiliate of
Professional Association of Diving Instructors (PADI)

ABBEVILLE PRESS PUBLISHERS
New York London Paris

Text and photographs: Roberto Rinaldi
Text of "The Fish of the Great Barrier Reef": Angelo Mojetta
Illustrators: Cristina Franco (dive sites); Monica Falcone and Patrizia
Pavanello ("The Fish of the Great Barrier Reef")
Editorial production: Valeria Manferto De Fabianis
Copyeditor: John Kinsella, Diving Science and Technology Corp.
Translation: Studio Traduzioni Vecchia, Milan
Layout: Patrizia Balocco Lovisetti and Clara Zanotti
Production editor: Abigail Asher
Text designer: Barbara Balch
Cover designer: Jennifer O'Connor

Library of Congress Cataloging-in-Publication Data
Rinaldi, Roberto
     The Great Barrier Reef dive guide /text and photographs, Roberto
Rinaldi : illustrations of the dives and maps, Cristina Franco.
        p.   cm.
     ISBN 0-7892-0456-8
     1. Deep diving—Australia—Great Barrier Reef (Qld.)—Guidebooks.
2. Deep diving—Coral Sea—Guidebooks. 3. Great Barrier Reef
(Qld.)—Guidebooks. 4. Coral Sea—Guidebooks.   I. Title.
GV838.673.A8R55   1999
919.4304'066—dc21   98-28648

THE
GREAT BARRIER REEF
Dive Guide

Page 1: A shining school of horned batfish (Platax batavianus). This fish can be recognized by its distinctive body, which is more elongated than that of other batfish species.

Pages 2–3: The enormous gorgonian sea fans at Flinders Reef reach into the void of the Coral Sea, where the sea bed plunges to more than 3,000 feet (1,000 meters).

Left top: Crevices cut into coral towers create strong currents that in their turn favor the development of soft corals.

Left bottom: A gorgonian sea fan at the mouth of a grotto may signal that the grotto has other openings and thus a continuous flow of currents.

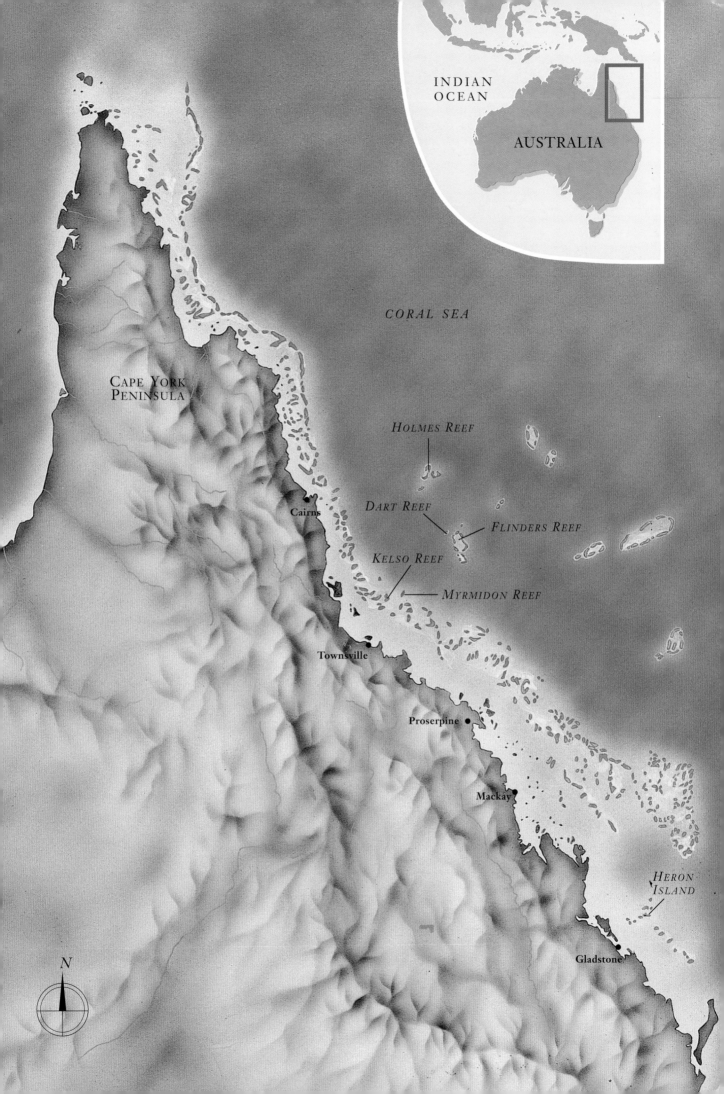

INDIAN
OCEAN

AUSTRALIA

CORAL SEA

CAPE YORK
PENINSULA

HOLMES REEF

DART REEF

FLINDERS REEF

Cairns

KELSO REEF

MYRMIDON REEF

Townsville

Proserpine

Mackay

*HERON
ISLAND*

Gladstone

N

INTRODUCTION

A detailed dive guide to the Great Barrier Reef would be a massive undertaking. It would be like describing what you would see on a walk across Europe—the flowers, the insects—the underwater life down to the tiny fish and crustaceans.

The Great Barrier Reef is 1,430 miles (2,300 kilometers) long and from 37 to 168 miles (60 to 270 kilometers) wide, with more than 2,500 isolated reefs. It is home to more than 400 coral species; more than 4,000 types of shellfish, crustaceans, and other invertebrates; and 1,500 species of fish, not counting reptiles and mammals. It lies in an immense ocean, full of fish and corals—a fascinating and varied underwater world that offers an infinite number of dives.

So, what is the scope of this work? It is not a list of the most beautiful dives in the Great Barrier Reef and the Coral Sea or even a list of our favorites. We describe a number of dives in a series of easy-to-follow itineraries, using the routes most commonly suggested by experienced tour operators.

A family visiting the mainland could take a one-day cruise with only two dives; a dedicated diver could take a cruise of three or four days. An enthusiastic diver, who set off for Australia with the firm intention of examining the sea beds of the Pacific Ocean, could take a long cruise to the farthest reefs. For a diving holiday without having to live on board for days, divers could

A. The coral formations along the Australian coast create an intricate labyrinth that reaches to the surface, sometimes passing it and creating sand banks or islands.

B. Fan-shaped gorgonians, chiefly of the Subergorgia *and* Melithaea *varieties, colonize vast stretches of the sea bed, especially where the walls are uneven and the currents constant.*

C. Small schools of fish circle in the water, reflecting the light with silvery scales that catch the attention of larger predators, attracted by the continuous glitter.

*D. Small barracuda (*Sphyraena *sp.) often form large schools that look like walls. The diver cannot guess what is concealed behind this live curtain.*

*E. Alcyonarians (*Dendronephthya *sp.) vaunt an astonishing richness of form and size. When the environmental conditions are favorable, they can colonize large stretches of the Barrier Reef.*

F. The light penetrating from the surface has made this hard coral assume a cuplike form ideal for producing nutritious substances through photosynthesis.

G. Constant currents transport more plankton, so the gorgonian branches grow bigger and denser.

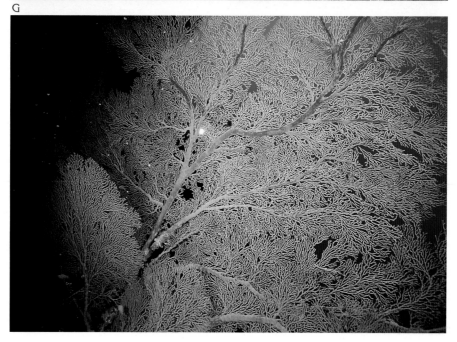

A. Near the sea bed by a grotto these two large cobra fish (Pterois volitans), with their fascinating but dangerous pointed fins, look for prey.

stay at an island resort. It is possible to choose from the itineraries to customize a vacation.

Each chapter of the book presents a sample itinerary. The number of dives included in a chapter depends on the duration of the stay. For instance, cruises to Flinders Reef usually last almost a week, while those to Holmes Reef generally last from three to four days, so we have described more dives at Flinders

B. A school of grunts closes ranks as the diver approaches. It is essential that divers on the Yongala *wreck behave well for the fish to remain confident with humans.*

C. A large stingray has temporarily left the sandy sea bed where it usually lives, perhaps to look for an area with more food.

D. This gorgonian and the arborescent colony of translucent alcyonarians grow very close to one another, witnessing not only the biological affinity of the two organisms, but also the fact that both feed on particles suspended in the water.

E. When this image was taken near the Yongala *wreck, the fish and turtles were scared by an approaching group of hunting dolphins.*

I

F

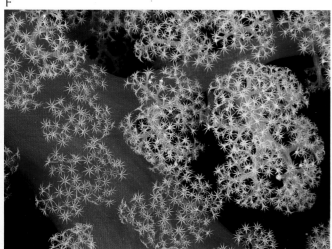

G

H

J

F. The arrangement of the polyp clusters of this soft coral is only apparently chaotic: each polyp occupies a precise space that does not obstruct the activity of the others.

G. This photograph of yellow coral blocks clearly shows the crown of tentacles in the center of which the mouth of the polyp opens. This is a voracious predator, despite its innocuous appearance and small size.

H. It is hard to see this tiny goby against the gorgonian branch; this is the environment where it finds shelter, food, safety, and a nest for its offspring.

I. This shrimp, which resembles a tiny lobster, moves carefully along the sea bed, inspecting the surroundings with its long feelers.

J. Anemonefish or clownfish (Amphi-prion perideraion) are often found close to the surface, but always sheltered from the force of the waves.

A. Some spectacular gorgonian sea fans project from the sea bed of Flinders Reef, a large reef lost in the immensity of the Coral Sea, where everything seems to grow much bigger than elsewhere.

than at Holmes. This book will be useful in planning your trip—a source of information before you reserve a bungalow in a resort or a cabin on a yacht. Once you have arrived, all the dives on the Great Barrier Reef, even if not exactly the same as those described here, will definitely be exciting.

D

A

B

C

E

B. Schools of large grunts are an almost daily sight by the Yongala wreck. The large ship has become a favorite spot for numerous fish that have conquered this unusual man-made reef.

C. This sea turtle seems to be as curious as the diver facing it. Unless threatened or disturbed, these animals easily accept the presence of humans.

D. The strange forms of these gorgonians indicate that this species is particularly suited to waters with strong currents. The

branches, united only at the base, do not offer resistance to the water flow.

E. Sometimes jacks and barracuda join in mixed schools, in areas very rich in fish, where they can live together without having to compete.

F. The giant grouper, often called potato grouper (Epinephelus tukula), confidently approaches the divers almost as if wanting to be caressed; this should, however, be avoided, in order not to remove the mucus that protects their scales and skin.

G. Snappers are one of the most common species of the coral barrier. During the day they prefer to gather and remain immobile in shaded areas.

G

F

H

H. A large barracuda lazily patrols the waters in front of the reef. These large solitary fish always elicit a reverential fear in divers. They certainly do not present a danger here, where there is plenty of prey.

I. Even in the clear waters of the Coral Sea a dive light or strobe is necessary to admire the beautiful colors of the gorgonians.

I

Environmental Dangers

Diving in Queensland is not dangerous in itself. As always, diving itself involves some risks and it is wise not to underestimate certain environmental factors. For instance, the water here is incredibly clear and you must continuously check your instruments to avoid going too deep. Also, currents are often very strong around the bommies and along the outer reefs of the Coral Sea. Try not to lose contact with the sea bed and avoid going too far from the walls along which you ascend to the surface. Stay close to the mooring rope to ensure that you can easily reach the boat. Always pay attention to the dive plan, observe the conditions of the sea from the boat, and listen attentively to the dive briefing.

Some potential dangers also lurk among the corals. These dangers are more theoretical than real—very seldom do divers get hurt by resting their hands on the spines of the stonefish or firefish. Most people instinctively avoid jellyfish. Still, it is a good idea to familiarize yourself with the appearance of fire coral and poisonous fish. Avoid all contact with corals and other organisms of the Barrier Reef, not just for your protection, but for the protection of the environment.

The risk of being bitten by a barracuda or moray or of being eaten by a shark is truly minimal. In our opinion, you should be most attentive in areas where fish feeding takes place. Fish have become accustomed to taking food from the hands of divers and may become a bit too confident and even frightening. Diving in Queensland is a marvelous and completely safe experience when you use some good sense, follow the advice of the tour guides, and most important, avoid overdoing it and making dives unsuited to your level of experience.

A

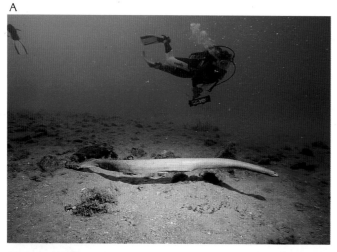

B

A. With poison stronger than that of the cobra, sea snakes are not exactly ideal diving companions. They will attack when touched or cornered.

B. This large stingray (Dasiatys sp.) has a robust spine connected to a poison gland on the upper part of the tail. Used as a lash in the case of serious threats, the tail and spine can be a dangerous weapon.

C

D

C. The cobra fish is common in all tropical waters, and most divers are probably familiar with it. Although its spines are very poisonous, it is sufficient to remain at a safe distance.

D. Striped catfish (Plotosus lineatus) can be fascinating, but remember to remain at a distance to avoid being wounded by the robust poisonous spines near the dorsal and pectoral fins.

Underwater Photography

A diving enthusiast who sets out on a journey to the sea of Queensland should certainly return home with beautiful images of this incredible submerged world. Tour operators in Australia often have good underwater cameras to rent for divers who don't own their own equipment. Amateur underwater video cameras are usually available and the divemaster on board can offer tips to beginners. In most cases, you can develop your precious roll of film on board, so you can try again if you don't get it right the first time. Watertight disposable instant cameras can be bought in many shops.

You can get good results with these when you shoot just below the surface on a sunny day, paying close attention to framing and composition.

It is worthwhile to emphasize some basic rules that may help inexperienced underwater photographers, who plan only to rent a camera for a few days, get some good photographs. Be careful when you are buying film. If possible, choose 100 ISO slide film. Once in the water, regardless of the length of your lens, never forget these two rules: (1) always choose a clearly distinct subject and avoid general scenes that lack impact and (2) try

A

B

C
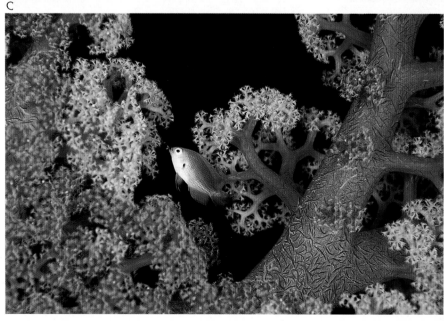

A. Even in the limited space at the top of this coral column you find a variety of micro-environments, each of which is colonized by different organisms, preferring currents, light, or shade.

B. The greatest difficulty for an underwater photographer is choosing a subject. However, the Australian coast is so rich in life that you can be sure to get interesting images.

C. To many small fish, such as this young chromis (Pomacentrus sp.), the colonies of large branched soft corals (Dendroneftidi) present an ideal habitat where they can seek refuge and find food.

to reduce the distance between lens and subject as much as possible. Plan to work at a distance of 2 to 3 feet (60 centimeters to 1 meter). Illuminate shaded areas with a flash and take care to aim the lens slightly upward at depths between 33 and 100 feet (10 and 30 meters). At these depths, apertures between f/8 and f/5.6 should guarantee good results. Set your lens to f/11 or perhaps even f/16 when you are closer to the surface on bright sunny days. Try some macrophotography—use additional lenses or extension tubes equipped with rods for framing and focusing at a distance. Good results are attainable, provided, of course, that you have chosen the subject with care and framed it attentively.

The situation is much more complex for expert photographers, who in the waters of the Great Barrier Reef and especially in the incredibly clear waters of the Coral Sea find infinite inspiration for splendid images. The type of photography that works best differs considerably between these two areas. The main differences involve water quality—it is generally more cloudy in the Great Barrier Reef— and the nature of the subjects. The Coral Sea is the land of giants: gigantic alcyonarians, gorgonians 15 feet (5 meters) wide, endless walls, oceanic fish, and so on. This submerged world seems designed especially for taking photographs of splendid subjects against a fabulous background with a wide-angle lens. The smaller life forms are equally fascinating, though. In our personal experience, we have always preferred to focus on environmental photography during the day and reserve our macrophotography equipment for night dives. Less than an hour under water is sufficient to finish an entire 36-exposure roll of film.

D. The photographer must show respect for the organisms of the sea. When you are taking macrophotographs very close to the sea bed, it is especially important to control your movements.

E. It is not easy to distinguish tiny organisms, such as this mimetic crustacean, among other creatures. However, macrophotography enthusiasts know the abundance of subjects concealed in every point of the barrier.

F. A specimen of Clark's anemonefish (Amphriprion clarkii) remains immobile near one of the numerous anemones with which it associates. This is one of the most common species; thanks to its territorial habits, it is very easy to photograph.

The Great Barrier Reef, on the other hand, is a mass of coral that continues as far as the eye can see, like an enormous mountain chain. It is very hard to render all this immensity on film. Try to include an element in the foreground, something that catches the viewer's attention and emphasizes the size of the background. Take the same film and equipment you would bring on trips to tropical countries. High-quality film and electric batteries are easy to find in Townsville and in Cairns, the main bases of departure for diving trips. Some materials can be bought on board the cruise yacht. This should, however, only be considered as an emergency solution. The electric current in Australia is generally 220 volts, but you often find areas designed specifically for recharging flashes and lights equipped with 110-volt sockets. The areas for rinsing and maintaining cameras are also usually quite well equipped.

Diving in the State of Queensland

The Great Barrier Reef develops along the coast of Queensland. All of the cruises sailing for the reefs scattered in the immense Coral Sea depart from this area. Underwater activities are governed by law in Queensland. Not only is a diving certification mandatory, but some technical aspects of diving are also governed by law. For instance, the law of Queensland states that you may not dive deeper than 130 feet (40 meters) and that the depth of a dive may not exceed that of a preceding one. You can find these rules in any diving manual, and they should not be considered a nuisance. They are clearly described and explained during the initial briefing on all dive tours. Do not forget your diving certification card!

There is no season when the weather prevents diving in Queensland. The average air temperature remains at about 77°F (25°C) in winter and 90°F (32°C) in summer. The peak diving season is from October to December, but from July to September is also excellent, if a bit colder. Water temperature also remains quite stable. It ranges between 73°F (23°C) and 82°F (28°C). Temperatures vary more in the shallow waters inside the Great Barrier Reef than in the deep Pacific Ocean around the reefs of the Coral Sea. For those who want to travel during the Australian winter, we recommend a well-fitting 3-mm neoprene wet suit with a detachable hood, especially if you intend to make three or four dives a day and

A. The coral barrier off the coast of Queensland creates a wide variety of environments. Shallow sea beds that sometimes surface when the tide is low alternate with winding channels and lagoons where you can dive in complete safety among swarms of fish.

B. Heron Island is surrounded by a large reef cut. A channel passes through the coral platform.

C. These yellow-eyed snappers (Lutjanus sp.) form dense schools that linger in the shade of the deeper coral towers.

finish with a night dive. A regulator with a submersible pressure gauge and an alternate air source are required. Many, but not all, operators equip visitors with a diving computer. This is an absolutely indispensable instrument when you make more than two dives a day. While it is possible to rent all equipment on location, we recommend that you bring as much as possible—wet suit, mask, fins, and computer. Usually

the buoyancy compensator jackets available for rent are of excellent quality and the suppliers reliable. If you choose to stay at a resort, two dives are usually scheduled per day, made on two trips on a small boat, with a night trip planned occasionally. Two dives are also made during the day trips departing from the main bases of Cairns, Townsville, and Port Douglas. Very big, fast catamarans take divers to a number of platforms permanently anchored inside the Barrier Reef. From here, small boats take you to the dive sites. On long cruises in the Coral Sea or inside the Great Barrier Reef, four dives are usually made per day. Three dives a day and one night dive are more than sufficient to enjoy your holiday and the splendid sea of Australia, even though almost all operators offer "unlimited diving" as part of their "all-inclusive" packages. Very accurate briefings precede all dives. Divemasters do not normally accompany dives unless, you explicitly ask for one. Australians are very careful with regard to the environment. Almost all dive sites have fixed moorings to avoid damage to the sea bed by anchors, and great emphasis is placed on ecological issues during dive briefings. Very seldom will you find two boats at the same dive site, and each diving

operator makes some rotation of the underwater routes in order not to expose one area to too much stress. The dives suggested by the operators suit all levels of experience, from the lowest to the highest. Dives inside the Great Barrier Reef are usually easier and suited to absolute beginners.

The incredible luxury and efficiency of some of the large yachts that serve diving charters deserve mention. There are big yachts that have spacious cabins with private bathrooms, and even some of the aluminum catamarans are very stable and roomy. Almost all the main operators offer advanced or specialized courses on board, and it is possible to rent underwater video or photographic equipment and develop your slides on board. Seminars on biology, slide shows, and films are often offered in the evenings.

F

G

D

E

D. Shallow sea beds rich in coral blocks are very characteristic of the Great Barrier Reef. The underwater life is luxuriant even in shallow waters.

E. This photograph of a diver, who stands out against the surface illuminated by the sun, shows the transparency of the waters in the Coral Sea.

F. The reef walls do not drop sheerly. They are interrupted by terraces inhabited by fish that live on the sea bed or dig lairs among the detritus.

G. The branches of gorgonians and alcyonarians are populated by numerous organisms. Molluscs, fish, and shellfish, such as those shown here, are perfectly at ease in this particular habitat.

The Great Barrier Reef off Cairns

N

LIZARD ISLAND

Cod Hole

RIBBON REEF #10

Pixie Pinnacle

CAPE
FLATTERY

Challenger Bay

RIBBON REEF #9

CAPE
BEDFORD

RIBBON REEF #5

Clam Gardens

Cooktown

RIBBON REEF #3

Steve's Bommie

Temple of the Doom

A

Agincourt

Although Australia clearly has more than the Great Barrier Reef to offer tourists, it is this natural wonder that defines the continent for scuba divers. The huge coral barrier isolates the coast of Queensland from the open sea. Throughout its breadth, between 35 and 165 miles (60 and 270 kilometers) from land, the Great Barrier Reef comprises an area of shallow sea beds characterized by coral blocks. Consequently, the areas nearest the coast have quite shallow and rather turbid waters, not very interesting to divers. Closer to the barrier proper, where an almost continuous belt of coral divides the internal water from the open sea, the situation improves progressively: the waters become clearer, and isolated reefs of varying size appear on the sandy sea bed. This is why the best way to discover the most beautiful corners of the Australian Great Barrier Reef is to board a cruise yacht and spend several days in the area where the ocean and the continent meet, diving on the first coral buttresses of the continental platform. Visibility depends on how exposed the dive site is to the ocean waters. Depth very seldom exceeds 130 feet (40 meters), and you usually dive along reef walls that rarely descend more than 50 feet (15 meters).

Some of the underwater explorations described in this book focus on the famous bommies; the name is aboriginal and widely used by Australian divers to indicate a coral tower that extends to the surface. Along the reef, corals heap on one another in seemingly endless elongated ridges. The bommies offer colorful sea beds, rich in alcyonarians and gorgonians, which are often surrounded by large schools of fish. This is partly because they grow in the sand where passes interrupt the continuity of the Great Barrier Reef. When you swim along the coral walls, you will be astounded by the incredible extension of these living structures, which have no equal in the world.

A. A school of snappers swims away from the lights divers use to illuminate the quiet shaded area where they usually linger. At night they begin to hunt actively for shellfish, fish, and molluscs.

B. The coral blocks create massive structures on which numerous other organisms settle; each of them enriches the already complex architecture of the reef by encrusting, attaching, or perforating and destroying the substratum.

C. Jacks (Caranx sexfasciatus) usually swim in schools by lagoon entrances or close to the precipices of reefs, making rapid incursions among small coastal fish, one of their favorite prey.

D. Sponges, coral blocks, and alcyonarians mix along the entire reef, according to precise patterns only partly known to humans.

E. The stocky branches of this acropora can easily resist the force of the waves. Even if broken, these coral structures can continue to grow if they find a suitable substratum.

F. The crown of thorns (Acanthaster planci) is one of the worst enemies of the corals. Crawling along the sea bed, its mouth rests on the delicate coral polyps, which it digests, leaving a trail of dead coral.

Agincourt Reef

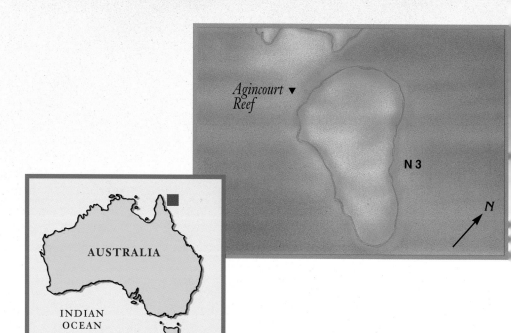

AUSTRALIA

INDIAN
OCEAN

Agincourt ▾
Reef

N 3

N

0 - 3 ft
0 - 1 m

23 ft
7 m

50 ft
15 m

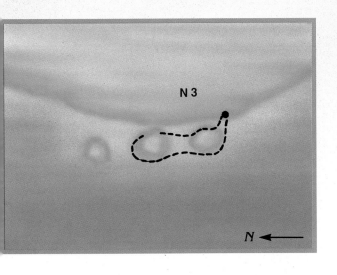

N 3

N ←

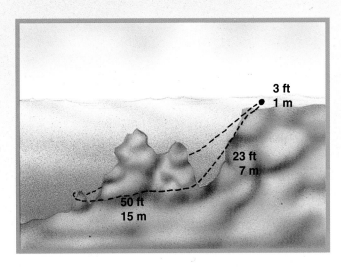

3 ft
1 m

23 ft
7 m

50 ft
15 m

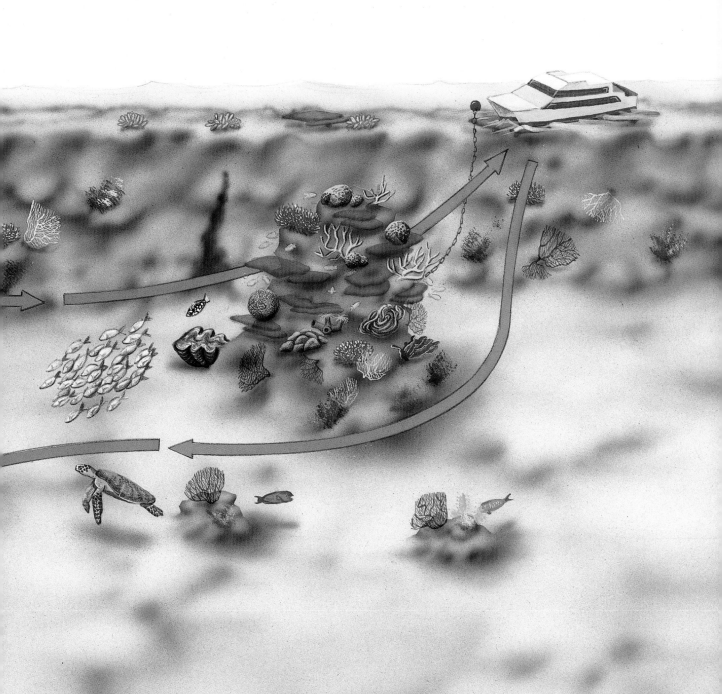

This is one of the first dives you can enjoy when sailing north from Port Douglas. There is a fixed mooring place on the inside of the reef, which follows an approximately north-to-south direction. On this dive you explore the walls of the reef by swimming north from the mooring. This is used as a check dive and often recommended at the beginning of *Supersport* and other yacht cruises.

This dive, which is well suited to beginners, never goes deeper than 50 feet (15 meters). Before reaching this depth, coral gives way to sand

C

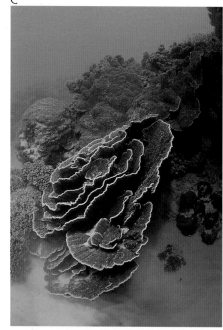

that drops gradually to a deeper sea bed. Be prepared for a fairly shallow dive where most of the beautiful sights are between 10 and 25 feet (3 and 8 meters). An infinite variety of hard corals welcomes you to the Great Barrier Reef. On top of the immense coral constructions you find numerous crinoids. In more shaded areas you see the calyxes of *Tubastrea*, particularly beautiful isolated coelenterates with pink calcareous calyxes that wait for night before they open their crown of yellow tentacles. Some small sea fans (*Melithaea* sp.) grow at about

A

D

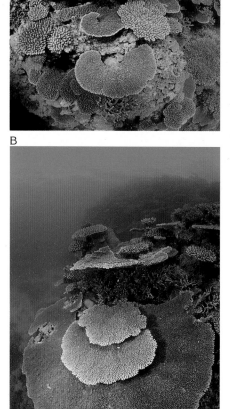

B

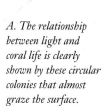

A. The relationship between light and coral life is clearly shown by these circular colonies that almost graze the surface.

B. These platform-shaped acropora seem to be the fruit of the efforts of a bonsai gardener.

C. These coral blocks of the Agaricidae family show a curious spiral growth that enables the colony to expand without obstructing the exposure to light of the new polyps, gradually produced by the fission of the old ones.

D. The carpet of sharp deer-horn acropora seems to ward off the diver, or at least advise him to control his movements so as not to damage the coral.

33 feet (10 meters), clinging to the western wall of the bommies. The most peculiar sessile organism in this area is certainly a large giant clam (more than 32 inches [80 centimeters] long) that rests on the sand at about 23 feet (7 meters) with its shell almost completely exposed. You can easily locate it between the first bommie immediately visible to the right of the mooring buoy and the

coral wall. The fish fauna is quite rich and consists of various species of coral fish, including chromis, triggerfish, parrotfish, and many snappers. Numerous cuttlefish and turtles live in this area, too.

PHOTOGRAPHY

Water conditions in this part of the Great Barrier Reef are not always excellent. While visibility is usually unlimited, the water is rich in suspended particles, which makes it appear opalescent. It is important to

bear this in mind when using a wide-angle lens. Photographs may lack intense colors and have a somewhat washed-out appearance. Take great care, therefore, to angle the light of the flash correctly, avoiding very intense and head-on illumination, and make sure that the flash is well behind the camera. A slight underexposure of the background makes the ocean appear more blue.

E. A crown of thorns (Acanthaster planci) *moves on the corals, its favorite food. After a massive invasion in the 1980s, the number of these starfish has returned to normal levels.*

F. A giant clam. These bivalves, which grow to be longer than 7 feet (2 meters) and can weigh more than 200 pounds (100 kilograms), have been subject to extensive fishing in the past, and have been in danger of extinction in many areas.

G. A large brain coral block partially colonized by an acropora with stocky, finger-shaped branches. Such behavior is frequent and represents the basis of the coral barrier's development.

H. This crinoid (Comanthina sp.) is distinguished by its bright yellow color, which stands out against the surrounding blue, especially when lit by a flash.

I. The presence of several crinoids often indicates constant currents and water rich in plankton, two factors ruling the life of these particular echinoderms.

Temple of the Doom

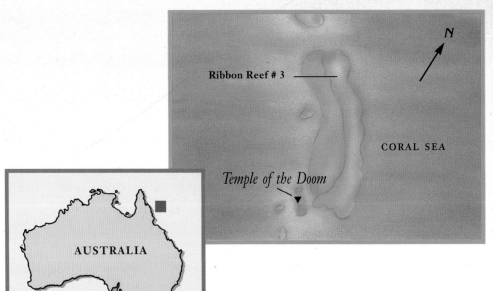

Ribbon Reef # 3

CORAL SEA

Temple of the Doom

AUSTRALIA

INDIAN
OCEAN

0 ft
0 m

65 ft
20 m

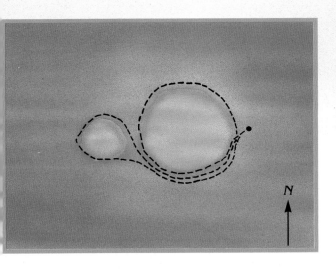

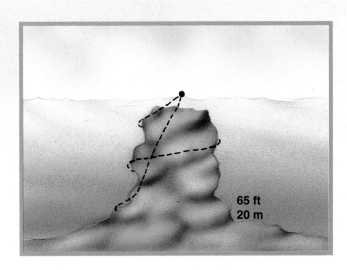

65 ft
20 m

A

B

C

Temple of the Doom is a small coral bommie, rich in life and color, inside the Great Barrier Reef. It is sheltered by the southern buttresses of Ribbon Reef #3. It is found in a particularly rich and interesting diving area, where it belongs to a small group of promising bommies that includes Fish Market, another wonderful dive that is not described in detail in this guide, but is worth investigating.

The dive starts from a boat moored on a coral bommie, near a coral tower that emerges from the sea bed at about 65 feet (20 meters)

D

and rises almost to the surface. The bommie's vertical walls are rich in sea life. Here, two bommies rise from a common base, one much smaller than the other. Technically, this is a standard dive: you immediately descend to the maximum depth and follow a spiraling route upward, exploring the coral walls on your way to the surface.

You swim alternately with and against the current when it is present. Swimming against the current is particularly interesting, because it is much easier to surprise the fish and get close to them. You will be amazed

A. Gorgonians often become the preferred substratum of crinoids. These echinoderms, characterized by long feathery arms, feed on organic particles and plankton that they filter from the water.

*B. Under the coral vaults or in grottos, it is quite usual to see glassfish or squirrelfish (*Sargocentron *sp.); these species are nocturnal and do not enjoy light.*

*C. Bluestriped snappers (*Lutjanus kasmira*) gather in numbers by large coral formations. When night falls, they scatter to hunt crustaceans and fish.*

*D. The head of a large moray (*Gymnothorax javanicus*) suddenly emerges from the tangle created by the uneven growth of corals.*

E. Descending the reef walls, you will see how corals predominate the first several feet, followed by more and more gorgonians and alcyonarians.

F. A grouper remains motionless near a diver. In frequently visited areas this fish gets accustomed to the daily presence of strangers.

*G. A whitetip reef shark (*Triaenodon obesus*) swims close to the sea bed in search of a place to hide. These sharks are not very active by day, when you see them inside grottos, half asleep.*

E

two coral towers. By the base of the two towers you find many species of coral fish—Moorish idols, angelfish, and butterflyfish. Occasionally, you may come across sea snakes, eagle rays, manta rays, and small reef sharks. You can see rays on the sandy sea bed, too.

PHOTOGRAPHY

Visibility is generally good at Temple of the Doom. The dense schools of yellow snappers and fusiliers make the most interesting and dramatic

photographic subjects here. The secret is to get as close as possible to the fish without making the school disperse. When this happens, all you get is a few small fish scattered in the image. So be very careful when you approach them against the current; control your breathing and breathe slowly and evenly until you have taken the picture, at which point the school will scatter and you will not get another chance.

H. The size of this stingray is emphasized by the diver beside it. It seems to move *effortlessly, slowly flapping its wide pectoral fins.*

F

G

H

by your first glance from the surface at the great abundance of fish at Temple of the Doom compared to other dives inside the Great Barrier Reef. You easily surprise dense schools of fusiliers and snappers, as well as pretty yellow-fin mullet. Descending along the walls, you find them to be rich and colorful: hard corals predominate at first, then alcyonarians, gorgonians, sponges, and crinoids become more numerous. You also find many beautiful anemones among the corals at various depths. Note the abundance of crinoids in the saddle between the

Steve's Bommie

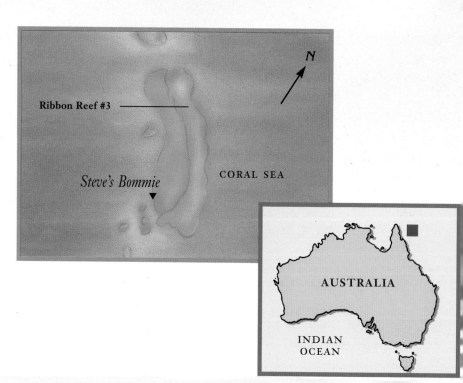

Ribbon Reef #3

CORAL SEA

Steve's Bommie

AUSTRALIA

INDIAN OCEAN

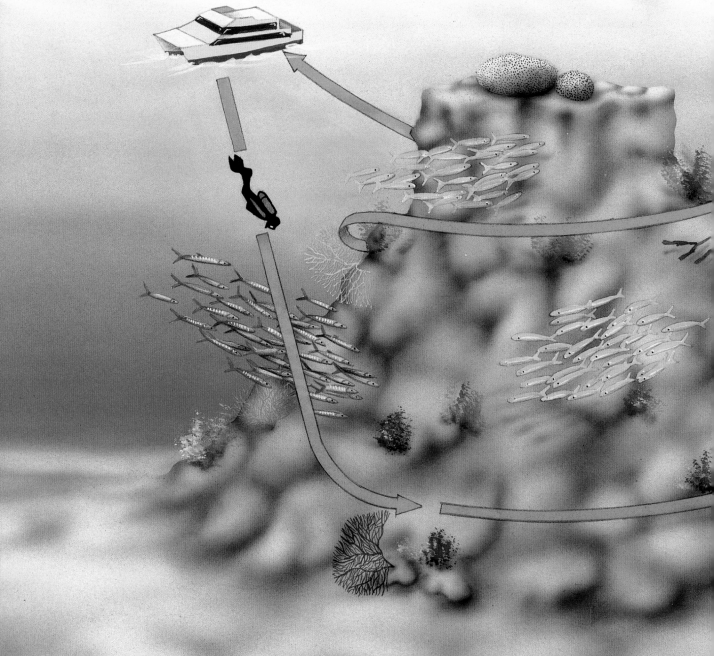

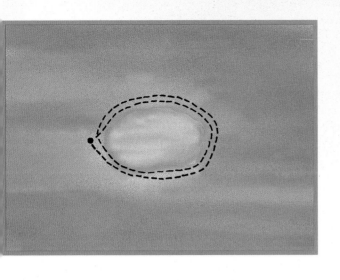

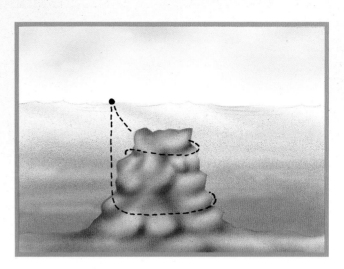

0 ft
0 m

15 ft
5 m

100 ft
30 m

This bommie is about half a mile (almost 1 kilometer) south of Ribbon Reef #3, in the pass between it and Ribbon Reef #2. The conditions are ideal for a good current, which means clear water. The best time to dive at Steve's Bommie is when the tide comes in, bringing ocean water through the pass to the Great Barrier Reef. Consequently, there is usually a strong current around the pinnacle, but the coral tower's morphology provides sufficient shelter.

The coral pinnacle rises steeply from about 100 feet (30 meters), where it rests on the sand. The top is about 15 feet (5 meters) from the surface and is distinguished by a large, round coral block with a smaller one not far away. Note how the various coral species divide the space. Massive forms of encrusted coral are very resistant to wave action, so the two large coral blocks

A. These two large coral blocks on top of Steve's Bommie are particularly massive.

B. Among the vertical corals of the barrier, the species with large, flattened colonies are typical of sheltered, deep environments, where the need for light is the most important factor.

C. A large giant clam (Tridacna squamosa), identified by the reliefs on the shell, opens its valves among the corals, showing its fleshy colored mantle.

D. At depths where the red light rays no longer penetrate, you find these large sponges with a laminar, sinuous structure. Only with artificial light do you discover their brilliant red color.

can easily survive on the top of the bommie, where slender branching corals would perish.

You will descend to the planned maximum depth immediately after entering the water, then circle the walls of the coral tower in an upward spiraling path. Near the bottom of the coral tower, its walls turn into a sloping surface that gradually meets the sand of the sea bed. At around 65 feet (20 meters), you see numerous sponges of the Verongida family. They appear green with slender structures that move softly in the current and the surf. A light or a flash reveals their real color, which is a pale pink. You will also see some other impressive coral formations, such as the laminar corals that emerge from 65 to 33 feet (20 to 10 meters). Continuing the ascent along a spiral path, you see the first schools of small yellow snappers. Many different anemones live among the corals, including a white species with a sphere at the tip of its tentacles. Don't forget to reserve sufficient air and film for the area near the surface.

A large school of big-eye jacks swims in the open waters. The stronger the current, the easier they are to approach. You may even succeed in swimming among them. Move against the current to avoid scaring the fish. While considerable experience is necessary to succeed in this, everyone is sure to enjoy trying.

PHOTOGRAPHY

Clear water, steep walls, and a rich selection of fish and benthic organisms are the ingredients of a photographer's paradise. Focus on the pink sponges during this dive. Photograph them against the sunlight to emphasize their delicate web and illuminate them a little with the flash. Remember to save half the roll for the school of jacks in open water. The secret here is to move carefully. Sudden, fast movements make the entire school flee, while a slow approach always gives good results.

E. *A group of yellow snappers, true to habit, lingers at 50 to 65 feet (15 to 20 meters), preferring more sheltered and shady areas of the sea bed.*

F. *Schools of jacks usually indicate that the waters are rich in fish and exposed to currents, which these powerful swimmers have no difficulty mastering.*

G. *Although they belong to two very distant groups in terms of taxonomy and evolution, the yellow crinoid and red gorgonia shown here share feeding habits.*

Clam Gardens

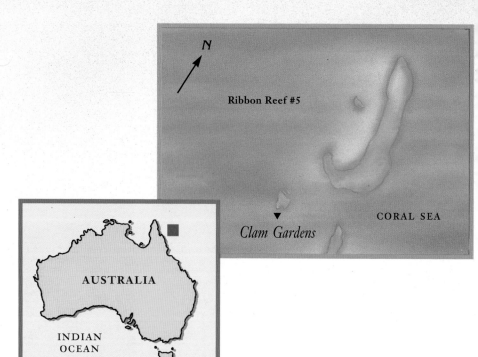

N

Ribbon Reef #5

Clam Gardens

CORAL SEA

AUSTRALIA

INDIAN OCEAN

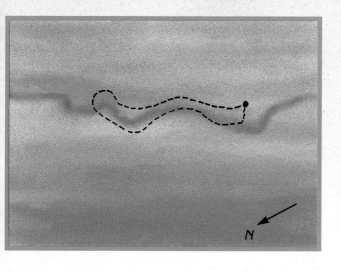

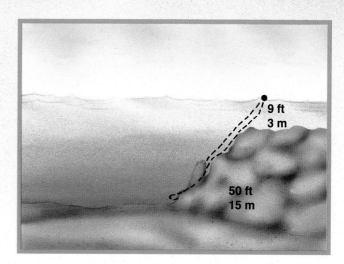

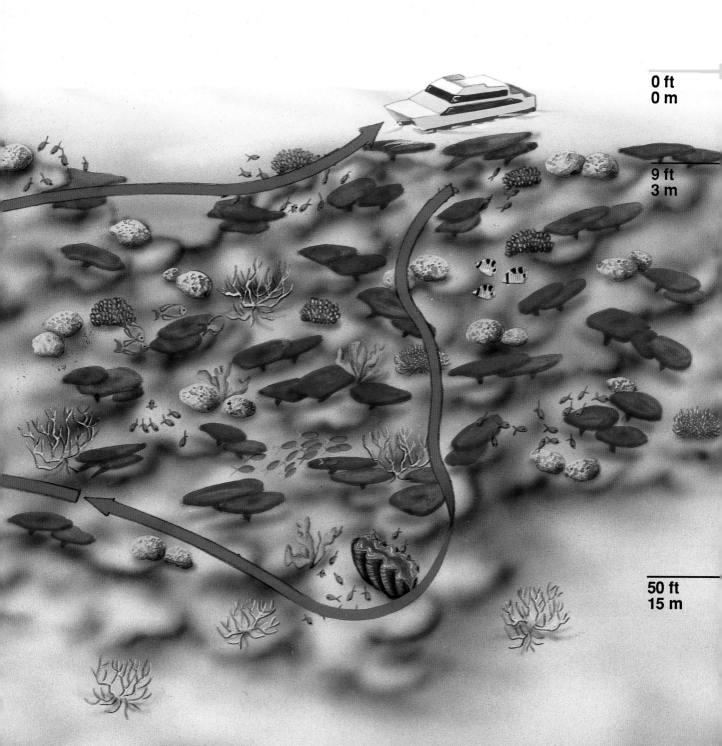

0 ft
0 m

9 ft
3 m

50 ft
15 m

Clam Gardens is located in the area of the Great Barrier Reef sheltered by Ribbon Reef, which divides the open sea from the area rich in bommies and other large coral structures. More specifically, we are close to the southern extremity of Ribbon Reef #5. The boat moors to a fixed buoy near the coral group, isolated on a sandy sea bed, that we are about to explore. The coral group is not very large, and you can swim for long stretches without fear of getting lost or being unable to locate the boat. During this dive you do not go very deep. Exceeding your no-decompression limits is not a problem, although divers should still plan their dive and stay within that plan.

You swim at depths from 15 to 50 feet (5 to 15 meters) in an environment formed of live coral towers and coral blocks. Sometimes the bright green of great colonies of soft corals of the Lobophytum and Sarcophyton families enlivens the scene. You can very often see dense schools of small coral fish leaving and entering their refuges among the colonies of acropora and montipora. The open pass between Ribbon Reef #5 and Ribbon Reef #4 is not far, so the water at Clam Gardens is generally quite clear, more so than at other dive sites inside the Great Barrier Reef.

As the name suggests, the most important characteristic of this dive is the large quantity of giant clams, clutched among the reef corals or isolated on the sandy sea bed. Researchers at James Cook University of Townsville, in collaboration with the Australian Military Marine, did an interesting experiment here some years ago. Their purpose was to see if giant clams could breed in captivity and be returned to the reefs—to protect them from

A. Constant currents have eroded narrow sandy corridors in the coral, which create a bright contrast, visible from afar, with the dark mass of reef.

B. These acropora colonies form a regular pattern around a coral pinnacle, providing light and shade to reef life.

C. Corals, gorgonians, and crinoids grow on top of one another in a continuous quest for space.

D. An unusual scorpionfish (Rhinopias sp.), with very variegated coloration, comes out of camouflage before the diver's camera.

extinction. The researchers were so successful that it became necessary to intervene a few years later. The newly introduced specimens and some of their offspring had to be transferred before the colony became too numerous, endangering the other sessile organisms living in the same area. The experiment revealed the incredible growth rate of these bivalves and their capacity to produce up to a billion eggs at one time.

E

F

PHOTOGRAPHY

Concentrate on the giant clams during this dive. Photograph them in their environment using a wide-angle lens and emphasize their most curious details with a macrophotography lens. Compose the frame of the environmental photographs to emphasize the mantle and the waved structure of the shell's edge. Pay close attention to your use of artificial light. Some giant clams stand out against a sandy sea bed and others are surrounded by hard corals. In both cases, the white sand or coral blocks near the brown mantle can result in an overexposed image. The elements that make the best macrophotographs are the mantle and its characteristic motifs.

E. This coral group owes its name, Clam Gardens, to the extraordinary abundance of giant clams. Their number increased drastically after experiments by University of Townsville researchers.

F. Giant clams are not very demanding in their choice of habitat. Most important is the presence of a hard substratum to which larva can cling during metamorphosis.

G. An enormous giant clam (Tridacna gigas) *emerges from the sand with its valves open. Notice, at the center of the mantle, the apertures of the siphons through which the bivalve continuously filters water.*

Challenger Bay

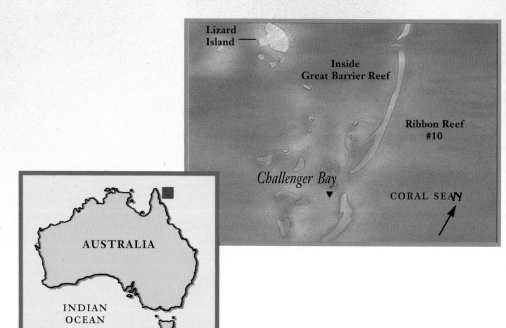

Lizard Island

Inside Great Barrier Reef

Ribbon Reef #10

Challenger Bay

CORAL SEA N

AUSTRALIA

INDIAN OCEAN

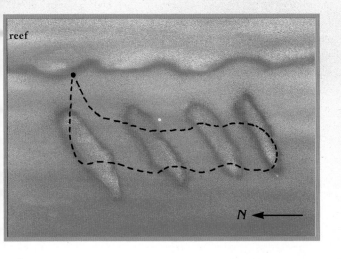

reef

N

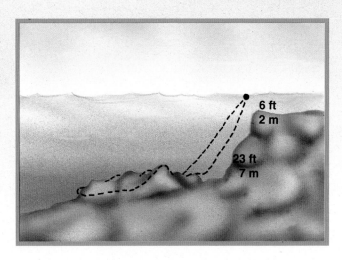

6 ft
2 m

23 ft
7 m

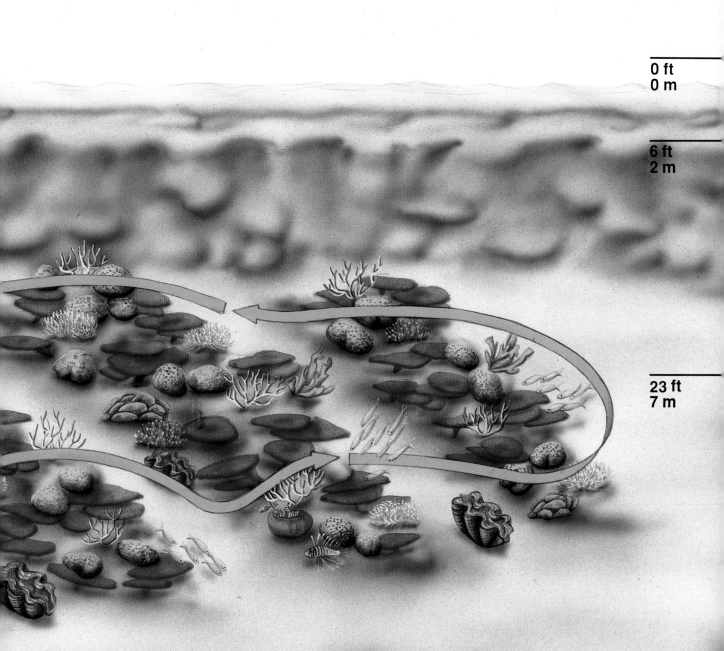

0 ft
0 m

6 ft
2 m

23 ft
7 m

A

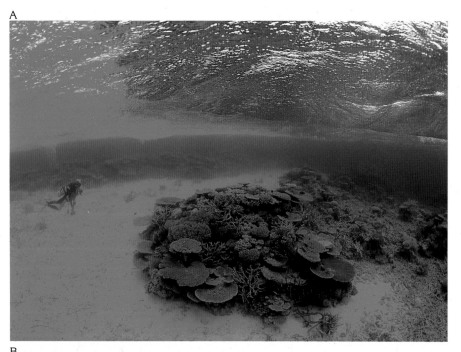

B

C

Challenger Bay is at the northern extremity of Ribbon Reef #9. It lies between Ribbon Reef #9 and Ribbon Reef #10, where Cod Hole, with its friendly giant groupers, is located. You are in the northern area of the Great Barrier Reef, well south of Lizard Island. It is difficult to give a practical description of this singular dive, and even more difficult to recommend a particular route winding among the delicate coral tongues reclined on the white sand. Perhaps hardest of all is to convince you that the waters of such a shallow lagoon, so poor in sensational encounters, can actually offer a very beautiful and enjoyable dive—an underwater stroll that globetrotter divers find hard to forget. At Challenger Bay you do not find any breathtaking walls that drop sheerly into the darkest abysses, you do not feel the thrill of meeting great oceanic creatures, and you aren't transported by the blinding colors of the enormous alcyonarians found in the Coral Sea. As soon as you put your head below the surface here, you discover a delicate coral garden with a series of marvelous lawns of a magnificently embroidered profile that decorate a carpet of pure white sand. Great, delicate umbrellas of acropora and fantastic structures of branched corals, resembling bushes bent by the wind and then petrified, strike the eye. Here and there, a few dozen small coral fish add color to this green and gray garden while some giant clams show off, completely isolated in the center of small islands of sand among the corals.

This is an easy and relaxing dive. You will never go below 33 feet (10 meters). You swim slowly for a long time without worrying about depth or time spent underwater. The limiting factors on this dive are

A. Even a small lagoon can be interesting. The mass of corals that grow isolated on the sand can protect numerous fish.

B. Seen from above, acropora umbrellas seem very robust and compact; they have an air of fragility when seen from below.

C. Flat acropora seem to challenge the law of gravity, with wide umbrellas supported by a slender stem. Only in sheltered places can these colonies develop fully.

F

G

D

E

D. This large giant clam is solidly anchored to detritus under the sand.

E. Small reefs with large acropora umbrellas surrounded by ramified corals grow on the sandy sea bed of Challenger Bay.

your air supply, which you should monitor carefully, and your desire to explore this magnificent corner of submerged paradise.

PHOTOGRAPHY

It is very difficult to render sensations in photography, to capture an environment rather than a detail. It is worthwhile to make an effort to work with a wide-angle lens here, carefully evaluating the natural light rather than using a flash. Given the shallow waters, we recommend taking some images very near the surface, using it as a foreground and a background to the coral garden below. This may be the right moment for inexperienced photographers to try to take some good images with the small disposable waterproof instant cameras that can be purchased in any shop in Cairns or even on the cruise boats.

F. Visiting sea beds close to the surface, you understand why the reefs are often compared to a garden. Massive tabular or ramified corals intertwine and mix, sometimes seemingly for aesthetic purposes only.

G. Acropora umbrellas are a distinctive element of areas of the barrier where the current is reduced and water transparency favors the development of flat coral blocks.

Pixie Pinnacle

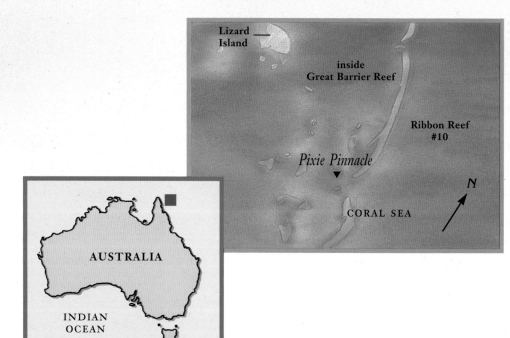

Lizard Island

inside
Great Barrier Reef

Ribbon Reef
#10

Pixie Pinnacle ▼

N

CORAL SEA

AUSTRALIA

INDIAN
OCEAN

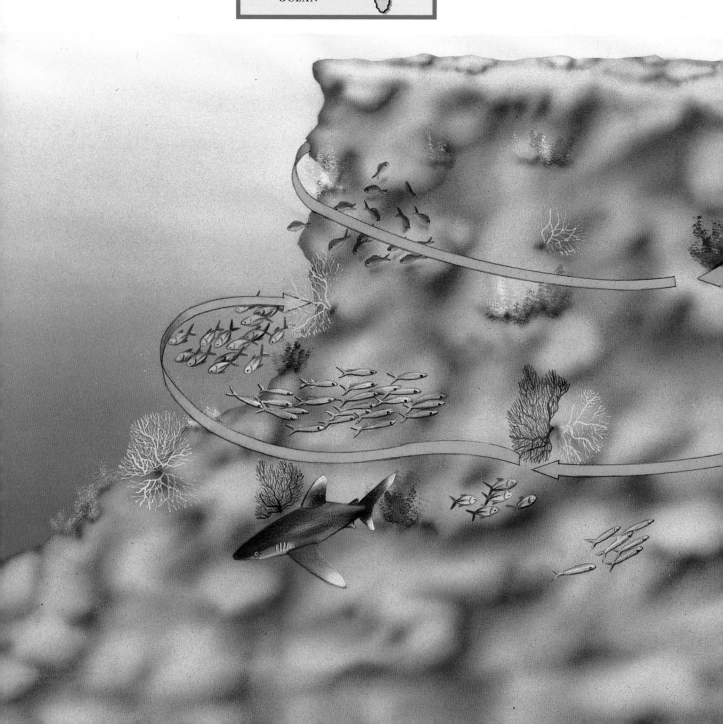

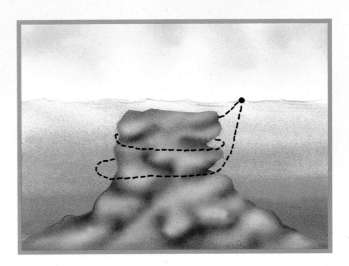

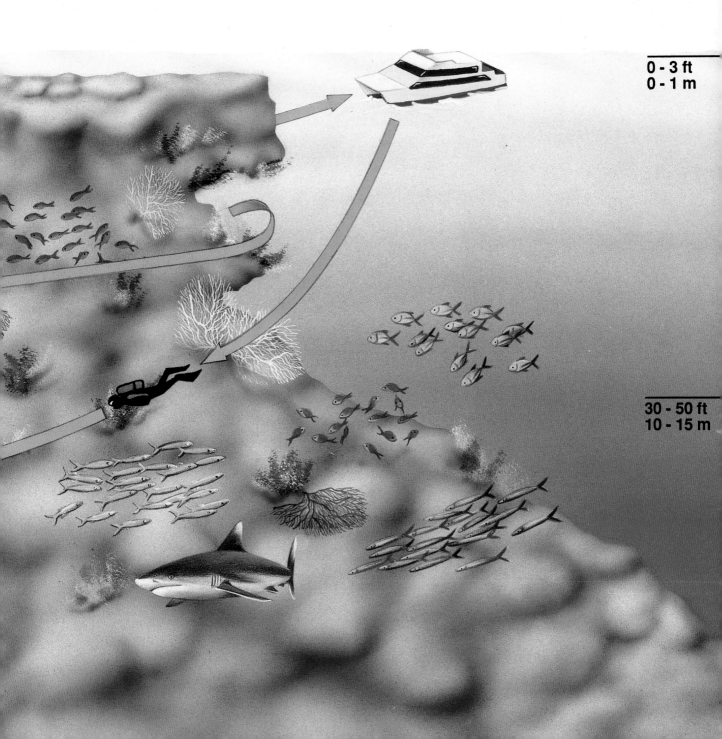

0 - 3 ft
0 - 1 m

30 - 50 ft
10 - 15 m

ixie Pinnacle is at the southern end of Ribbon Reef #10, famous for the groupers of Cod Hole at its northern end. The coral pinnacle you are about to explore rises from a sea bed in the open pass between Ribbon Reefs #9 and #10 from about 100 feet (30 meters) almost to the surface. Pixie Pinnacle is, therefore, exposed to the ocean current that enters the Great Barrier Reef at that point. The probability of good visibility is excellent. There is a fixed mooring just below the Ribbon Reef. The pinnacle is behind the mooring, anchored between the

B

the area where the vertical wall meets the sloping surface.

The dive begins by circling the coral tower. You immediately realize that one side is particularly rich in benthic life. The great richness of small sea fans, alcyonarians, countless crinoids, anemones, whip corals, and soft corals of different kinds is extremely evident. There is a great abundance, too, of small colored fish—anthias, chromis, and yellow snappers. The location is also good for spotting schools of jacks, barracuda, and surgeonfish. This is certainly one of the most beautiful

A

C

upper part of the shallow and the Ribbon Reef. The diameter of the top of the tower is about 33 feet (10 meters) and rises to about 3 feet (1 meter) from the surface. The walls drop vertically to a depth of from 33 to 50 feet (10 to 15 meters). From this point the sea bed becomes an even, inclined coral surface that meets the sand at about 100 feet (30 meters). The general appearance is that of a very wide cone topped by a regular cylinder. It is not worthwhile reaching the sandy sea bed: the most beautiful sights are found between the summit and 50 feet (15 meters), especially in

D

A. The streamlined bodies of the jacks form a column in the water, on the lookout for prey or bigger predators.

B. A giant clam with open valves shows one of its siphons. Contrary to many legends, these molluscs are too slow-moving to trap divers.

C. The giant cuttlefish is one of the surprises of the coral Barrier Reef. Capable of fleeing rapidly with jet movements, this cuttlefish remains at a safe distance from the diver.

D. The tangle of these crinoids' erect branches makes them resemble gorgonians. They are actually echinoderms capable of moving on the sea bed and even swimming short stretches, moving their feathered arms rhythmically.

E. A large coral tower, whose only living part is the surface, is home to alcyonarians, gorgonians, sponges, algae, and ascidians.

F. Encrusted corals adapt their form to the movement of the substratum they grow on; it is covered by a hard carpet from which the coral polyps project.

G. The upper part of the wide tips of deer-horn acropora are almost always lighter than the rest of the structure. This is due to the presence of new, more delicate and rapidly growing polyps.

H. A crevice in the reef wall gives rise to a more intense current, which promotes the rapid development of gorgonian sea fans.

E

F

G

dive sites inside the Great Barrier Reef, because of the generally excellent visibility, the luxuriant submerged walls, and the spectacular form of the pinnacle. Whenever the weather is suitable, Pixie Pinnacle offers splendid opportunities for outstanding night dives.

PHOTOGRAPHY

It can be quite difficult to choose the right lens before entering the waters at Pixie Pinnacle. The clear water and spectacular seascape suggest an

H

extreme wide-angle lens, while the abundance of fish calls for a less wide lens. On the other hand, the large variety of small life forms suggests the use of a macro lens. We suggest opting to focus on the fish and the numerous medium-sized organisms that cover the walls, such as the beautiful crinoids or the delicate branches of sea fans.

Cod Hole

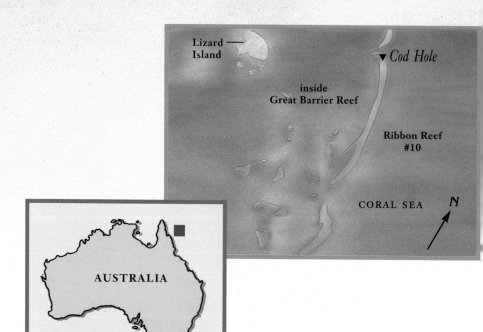

Lizard Island

Cod Hole

inside
Great Barrier Reef

Ribbon Reef
#10

CORAL SEA

N

AUSTRALIA

INDIAN
OCEAN

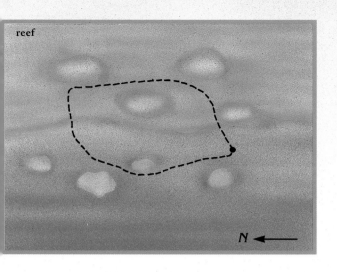

reef

N ←

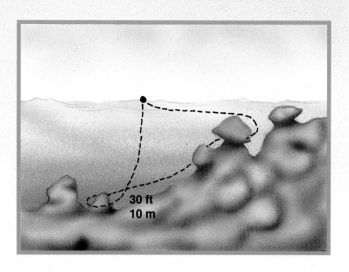

30 ft
10 m

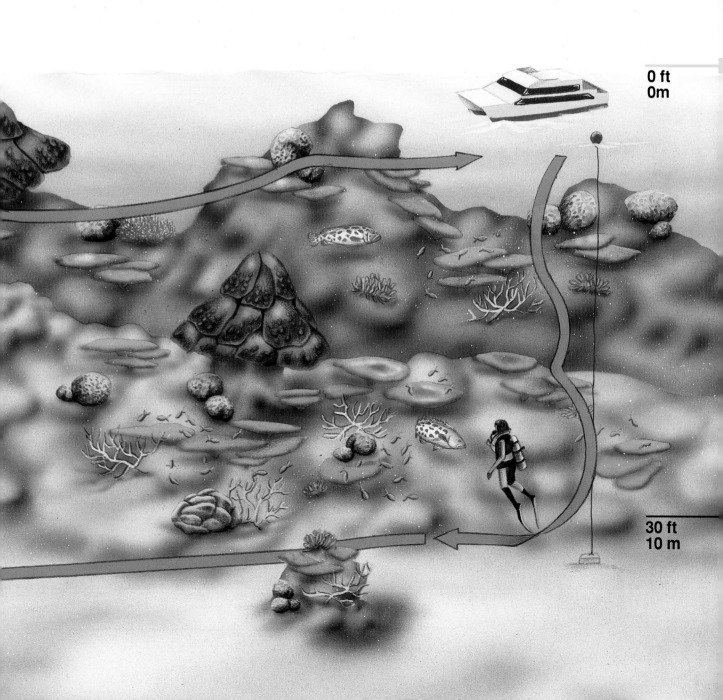

0 ft
0m

30 ft
10 m

*A, B, C. The potato
groupers (Epineph-
elus tukula) are the
main attraction for
divers; corals are
a secondary draw.*

*D. Shortly after enter-
ing the water, divers
are approached by the
large groupers, confi-
dent and curious, that
live in these waters.
They are accustomed
to the presence of
humans and even more
enticed by the food
offered them.*

Cod Hole is one of the most famous dive sites in the Australian Great Barrier Reef. A large family of tropical giant groupers, particularly used to humans, lives here. You are off Lizard Island, exactly on the borderline between the Great Barrier Reef and open sea. The diving spot is slightly inside the open pass between the northern extremity of Ribbon Reef #10 and the southern part of a nameless reef.

The highlight of this dive, clearly, is the encounter with the large groupers that live on the sea bed. So don't look for splendid gorgonian fans or brightly colored branches of alcyonarians, because you won't find any. Follow the divemaster along the mooring rope to the sandy sea bed at about 33 feet (10 meters). The groupers will soon approach. Between 5 and 12 enormous speci-mens, weighing from 175 to 440 pounds (80 to 200 kilograms), begin to circle with a lightness and elegance that belies their size, waiting for the food kept by the divemaster in a special closed container. A few seconds later the show begins: the enormous fish approach to a few inches from your face, sucking up

A

C

B

the offered food with a powerful movement of their mouths.

The sight of such large and friendly animals is fascinating. You may feel you are dealing with tame animals and want to touch and caress them, but be careful. A mucus which protects their skin from parasites covers their bodies. It is very easily removed by even a light stroke of the hand, especially if you wear gloves. Limit yourself to enjoying the incredible sight, taking photo-graphs and shooting videos, without trying to touch the animals. After you have fed the groupers, it is worthwhile to set off for a trip around the reef. You will probably discover some enormous moray eels, who are frequently uninvited guests at the groupers' meal. Then you can visit your large new friends in their dwellings, sheltered by large coral blocks. Here you can observe the natural life conditions of the groupers, who certainly do not spend all their time circling divers.

PHOTOGRAPHY

Equip yourself for environmental photographs. You are only a few feet under the surface so the generally good visibility and excellent light in this location allow any lens to be used successfully. A 35-mm Nikonos, for instance, is perfect for close-up images of a grouper's snout, 20 mm is suitable for shooting the entire animal, and 15 mm enables you to shoot the whole scene. Just remember to evaluate the environmental light correctly and use the flash only to lighten the shadows to avoid overemphasizing the inevitable suspended particles. Don't miss the opportunity to photograph the groupers in their natural habitat, minus the presence of divers with fish in their hands. The fish will obviously be less trusting and your task more difficult, but the results will make your efforts worthwhile.

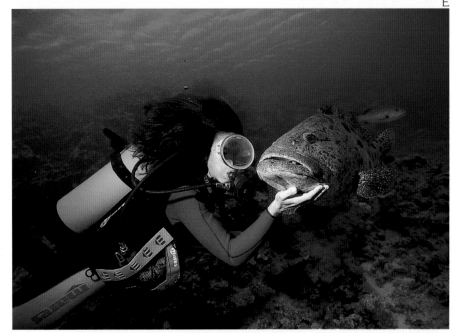

E. The temptation to touch these fascinating, seemingly tame, animals is very strong. However, resist this impulse, to avoid damaging the delicate skin of the fish by removing the protective mucus.

F. It is hard to describe the sensation of being so close to fish that weigh up to 440 pounds (200 kilograms) and grow to be almost 7 feet (2 meters) long.

Heron Island

This is a beautiful little coral island 985 feet (300 meters) wide and 1,970 feet (600 meters) long. Seen from a plane, it resembles an emerald set among extended coral reefs. Like a huge cruise yacht moored on the reef, Heron Island offers a strategic location to dive in the central section of the Great Barrier Reef. The reef is 45 miles (70 kilometers) from the mainland, but from Heron Island, you can dive on reefs that would be otherwise inaccessible with the utmost comfort and the least effort.

A modern resort and a biological research station have been built on the island. In fact, Heron Island is a bird sanctuary, and numerous turtles come here to lay their eggs. It really

A. Seen from a plane, Heron Island resembles a deep green gem set among extended coral reefs. The signs of human presence are discreet and well concealed among the vegetation.

B. The stretch of sea separating the island from the coast is studded by reefs that graze the surface and create an intricate labyrinth that is hard to navigate at low tide unless you are familiar with the passes.

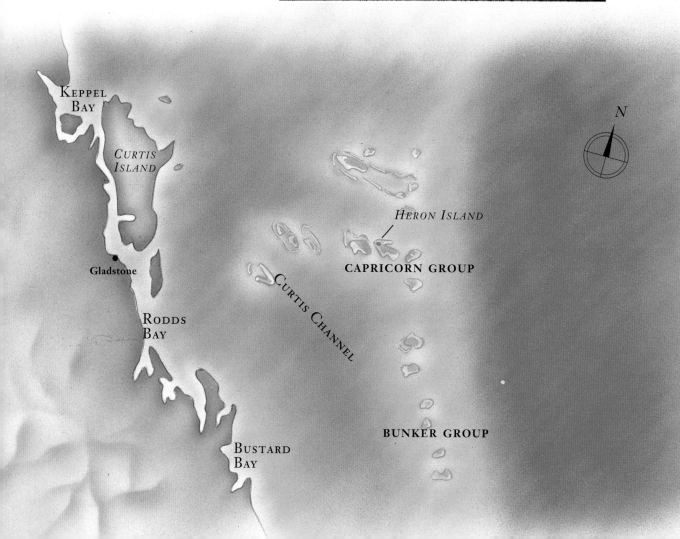

is worthwhile visiting Heron Island during the turtles' nesting period (between November and January). Researchers on the island even accompany tourists on turtle watches and give very interesting narratives.

Heron Island boasts about 10 main dive sites along with other, less important ones. The dives are generally quite easy and suited to all levels of experience. The dive center on the island guarantees excellent assistance during boat trips, and you can stay in the resort instead of spending a whole week on a yacht. Heron Island is particularly recommended for beginners.

C

Two dives are scheduled per day, starting by boat from the beaches near the main landing pier. It only takes a few minutes to reach the main sites. Underwater you will discover a beautiful environment, with rich and healthy corals and generally good visibility. There are few alcyonarians, while the gorgonians are more abundant, especially the beautiful, intensely red, scaled *Melithaea* species. It is common to encounter turtles, barracuda, and other oceanic species. Be sure to include a dive at Heron Bommies while you are here.

D

E

F

G

C. The vegetation on Heron Island includes a large variety of species, some reaching a height of 33 to 50 feet (10 to 15 meters).

D. As you approach Heron Island, the water becomes lighter and you encounter a barrier of trees that almost reaches the sea.

E. The Australian coast seems to become thinner and thinner before it disappears in the ocean from which Heron Island emerges.

F. The coral surfaces create a hard frame around the coral sand that surrounds the island, the result of erosion of the immense surrounding barrier.

G. The practically uncontaminated beaches of Heron Island are ideal for turtles, who come here to dig their nests and hide their eggs during mating season.

Heron Bommies

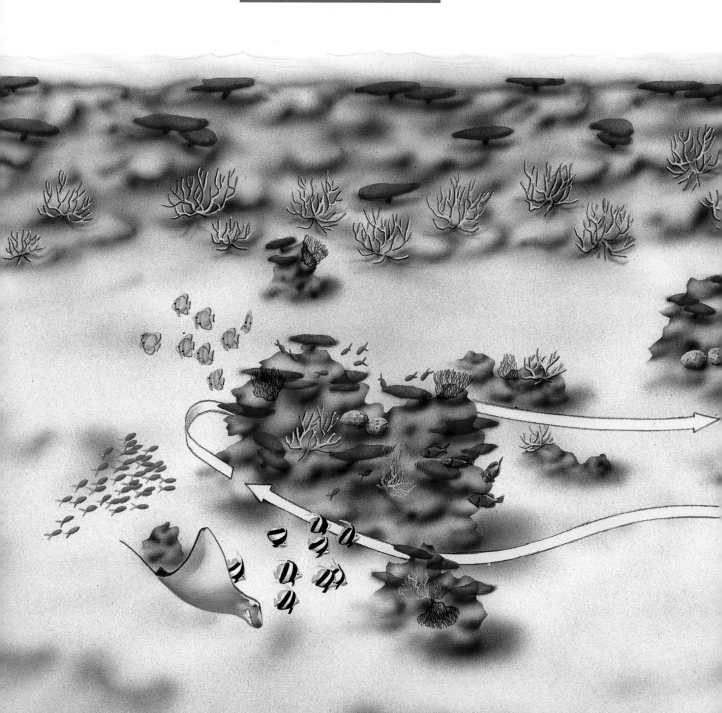

CORAL SEA

blue pool

Heron Island

lagoon

Heron Bommies

Wistari
Reef

AUSTRALIA

INDIAN
OCEAN

N

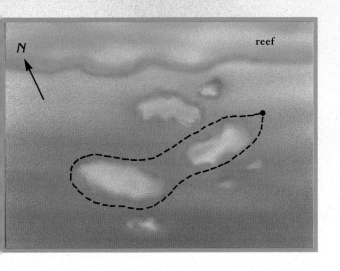

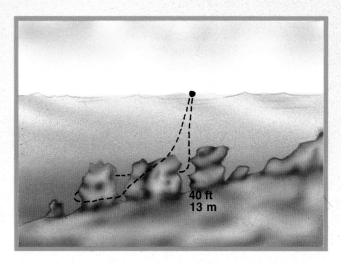

40 ft
13 m

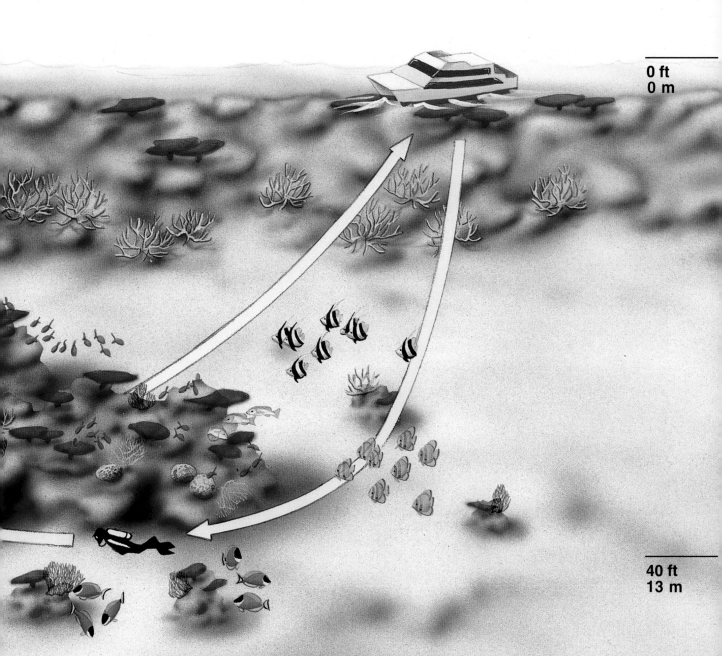

0 ft
0 m

40 ft
13 m

A. Colonies of acropora, with typical ramifications resembling branched horns, can cover large stretches of the barrier, thanks to their rapid growth and ability to survive after having been broken.

B. A spotted humped grouper (Cromileptes altivelis), *with its distinctive concave profile and densely speckled livery, is usually found in closed areas where the water is not very clear.*

C, D, E. The yellow-eyed or hussar snapper (Lutjanus adetii) *is one of the most common species along the coral coasts of Australia. They form large schools, scattering by night to hunt. The snappers linger in the shelter of the coral towers, their snouts facing the main current. When the light is too intense the snappers gather in shady areas of the reef, where it is easy to find and approach them.*

A

B

This dive site is very close to the ferry dock that connects Heron Island with Gladstone, just by the outlet of the artificial channel that cuts through the coral platform. You are at the western tip of the large reef that surrounds Heron Island, facing the channel between it and Wistari Reef. Heron Bommies is truly one of the most beautiful and enjoyable of all the dive sites offered by the very rich sea beds of the island. Although it is not of completely natural origin, the incredible confidence of the fish makes it a wonderful dive. In fact, hand feeding has been practiced here for many years.

The main reef terminates in a rich growth of ramified corals that reaches the sandy bottom. The sediment slopes softly to depths that soon exceed 33 feet (10 meters). Not far from the point where the branching corals end, you find a series of coral bommies, about 10 in all, 3 of which are particularly large. What makes this dive site interesting is not so much the coral forms as the incredible abundance of fish. Among the corals you meet numerous batfish, Moorish idols, butterflyfish, and barramundi (characterized by their peculiar profile). You will be especially intrigued by a very dense school of snappers with pointed snouts and eyes circled with yellow. They stay still, gathered in close ranks, sheltered from a slight current by the top of the lower coral towers. They really are a very beautiful and fascinating photographic subject. Accustomed to taking food from the hands of divers, they are not concerned with your presence, merely leaving lazily when the distance really becomes uncomfortable. Unless, of course, you bring something to offer them.

At the opening of the two small tunnels that cross one of the bigger bommies, you find two beautiful moray eels, called Fang and Harry by local divemasters. Swimming toward the external bommies, you may run into areas swept by the current that enters the channel between Heron Island and Wistari Reef. This current does not present a problem, as you can always find shelter behind some coral structure. On the contrary, it may provide a splendid surprise because it is not uncommon to come upon beautiful manta rays.

PHOTOGRAPHY

During this dive you concentrate on the fish—the snappers in particular. We recommend an average wide-angle lens, with the classic 20-mm Nikonos being ideal. Spot the school of fish gathered in the shelter of a coral tower, fix the flashes, and determine the exposure and distance from which you intend to take the picture. Then approach the coral and swim around the tower, unseen by the fish, and surprise them by appearing just as they leave their last hiding place. Cover the last few feet swimming slowly without making sudden movements and controlling your breathing, while ready to take the picture. As soon as the first fish begins to move, shoot without hesitation until the school scatters. You will have to repeat the maneuver for another image once the school has gathered again.

Gorgonia Hole

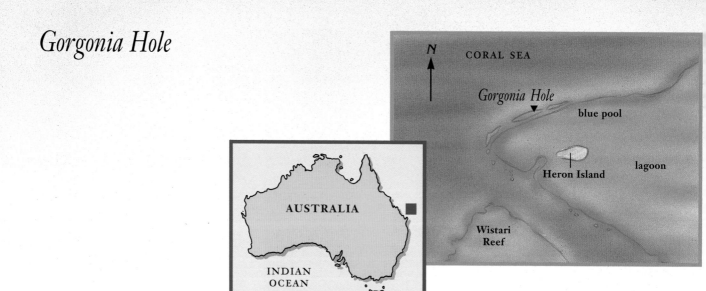

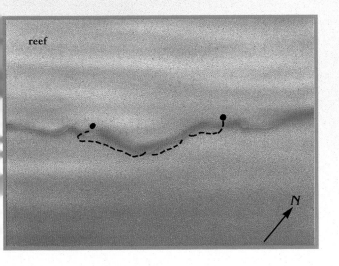

reef

N

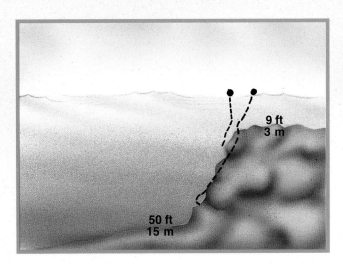

9 ft
3 m

50 ft
15 m

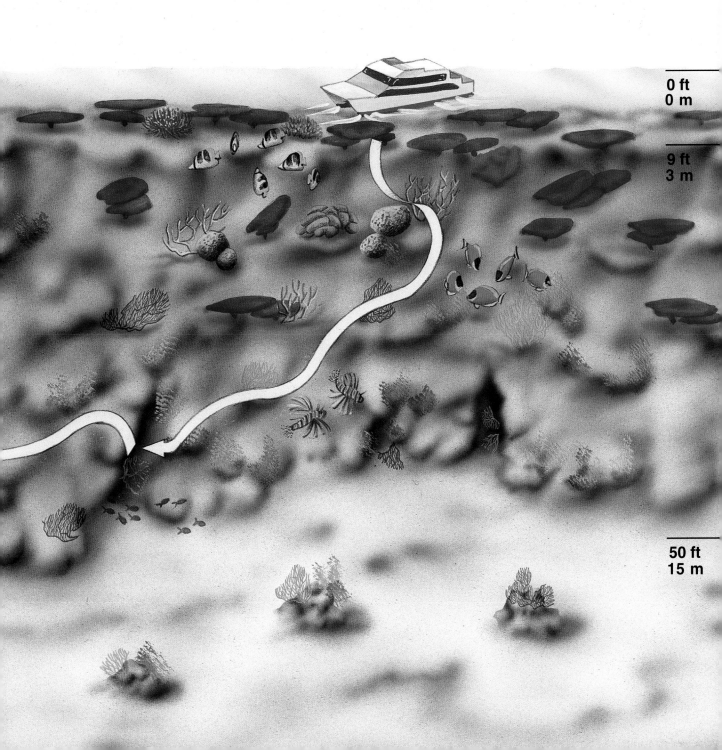

0 ft
0 m

9 ft
3 m

50 ft
15 m

Gorgonia Hole, one of the most famous dive sites at Heron Island, is north of the reef in the western sector. It is generally preferable to dive in these waters during high tide, when you can navigate the reef from the island. Dives here do not descend deeper than 50 feet (15 meters). You explore the steep coral wall that connects the upper part of the reef with the sandy sea bed. It is scattered with isolated corals and

A. Blocks of coral that project from the sandy sea bed become an ideal substratum for the growth of gorgonians, which attach to rigid surfaces.

A

B

C

D

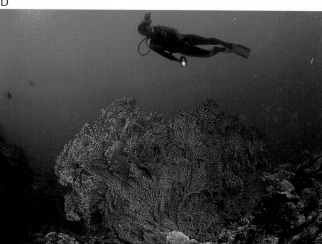

small groups of coral blocks. You generally only move in one direction on this dive, and the boat does not drop anchor. You swim along a long stretch of the beautiful wall without having to return along the same route. There are very jagged corals, cut by recesses, fissures, and small grottos. In these cavities, you find the most peculiar feature of this stretch of sea bed: the luxuriant

B. Cavities and crevices open along the jagged wall of the reef; here you find numerous gorgonians of various species, recognized by their ramifications and dimensions.

growth of small, brightly colored organisms. Countless small red and yellow gorgonian sea fans, alcyonarians of intense hues, numerous nudibranches, starfish, and sea urchins, and an infinite number of shellfish, such as crabs and shrimp of various kinds, make their home here. A large number of coral fish also hide among the recesses in the corals. In particular, there are numerous firefish with long poisonous fins, butterflyfish, Moorish idols, snappers, and small barrier groupers. At the point where sand and coral meet, hidden under the base of the wall, it is common to startle gigantic turtles, especially during the mating season. The turtles here are usually green *(Chelonia mydas)* and hawksbill *(Eretmochelys imbricata).* In these waters, it is not uncommon to witness two turtles mating, locked to one another in open water. Divers need to watch their air consumption and no-decompression limits, but the shallowness of this area allows you to make long dives at Gorgonia Hole, enjoying a pleasant and interesting exploration of the submerged world.

PHOTOGRAPHY

This is an ideal place for close-ups of small, brightly colored creatures, enlarging them with your special lens. Many underwater photographers find that the colors and bizarre forms of the subjects are sufficient to produce successful images. Framing your subject is fundamental to getting a good result. Pay close attention to this factor, especially if you are using an underwater reflex camera that enables you to control the image with precision.

C. Sometimes the anemones with which the clownfish associates can grow to considerable size, providing shelter for large fish families.

D. Gorgonian sea fans are the main attraction of Gorgonia Hole.

E. A pink anemonefish or clownfish (Amphiprion perideraion) is partially concealed among the tentacles of an anemone (Heteractic magnifica).

F. A large stingray swims away, flapping its fins and waving its tail. Note the lower fold that represents the anal fin.

G. A school of glassfish moves in the shade of a grotto, reflecting the flashlight like a mirror.

Hole in the Wall

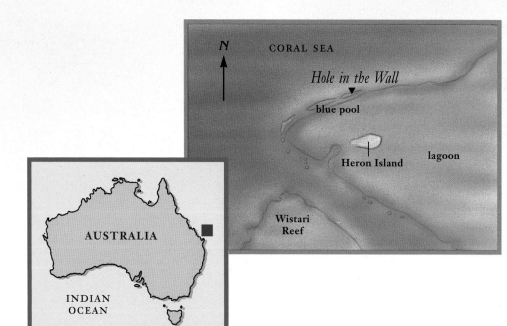

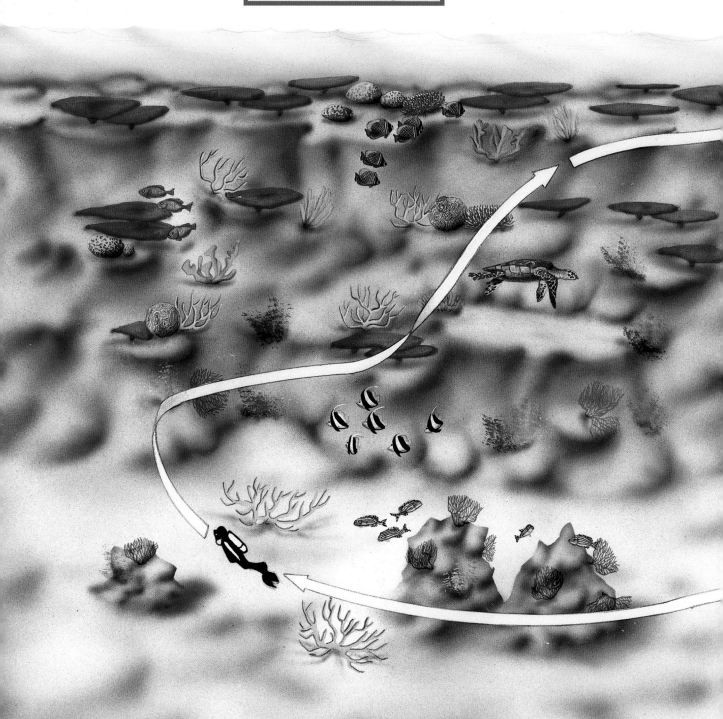

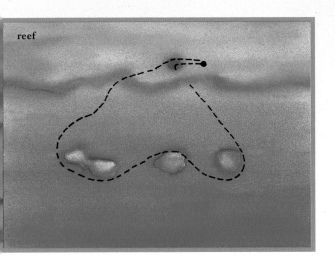

reef

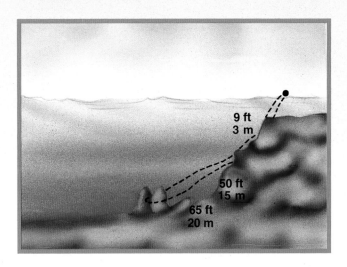

9 ft
3 m

50 ft
15 m

65 ft
20 m

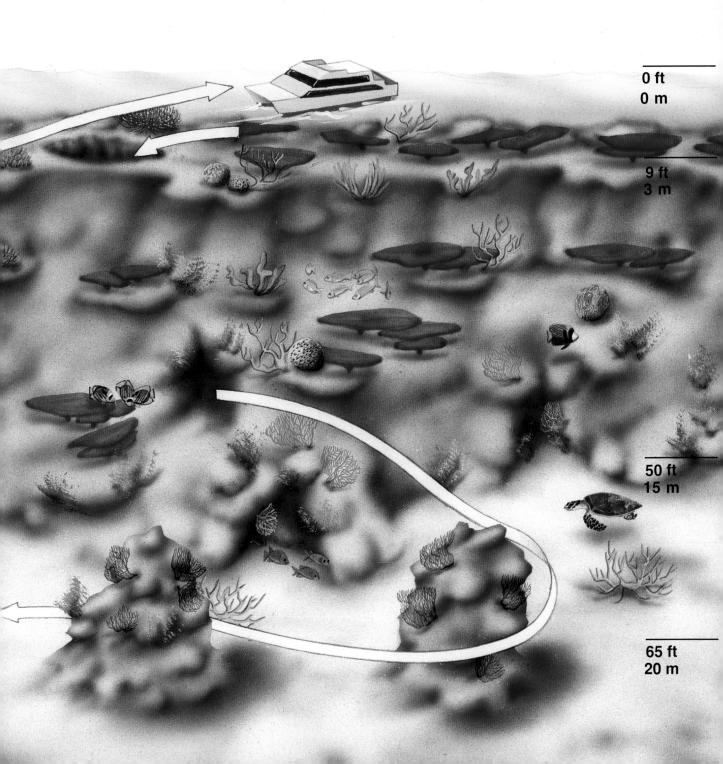

0 ft
0 m

9 ft
3 m

50 ft
15 m

65 ft
20 m

This is another dive in the northern area of Heron Island reef, some 325 feet (100 meters) east of Gorgonia Hole. As at Gorgonia Hole, high tide considerably simplifies navigation, enabling you to swim above the coral surface. Here you can reach depths of nearly 65 feet (20 meters) to explore a varied sandy sea bed, somewhat enriched by the presence of many small bommies. This dive owes its name to a hole in the coral platform, which leads to a short tunnel that opens in the center of the wall. The passage is large enough to let two divers pass at one time. The reef is particularly rich at this point, both along the wall and on the sea bed, which is scattered with small bommies and isolated corals. Here you find large, often massive, coral blocks, brain corals of almost perfectly spherical form, and soft corals, small colored alcyonarians, and gorgonians, especially of the *Melithaea* species. Crinoids are numerous, especially black ones, which prefer to grow on the acropora and gorgonians. There are many open passages in the corals and deep fissures rich in barrier fish and benthic organisms. The many small bommies scattered on the sand deserve a visit: they are rich in small gorgonians and colored alcyonarians. It is common to come across large turtles in open water or hiding in the recesses between sand and coral.

PHOTOGRAPHY

You should try your luck taking photographs of the turtles here. Use a medium wide-angle lens and set out in search of the reptiles, keeping an eye on the free water toward the open sea. The turtles are often found in recesses between the sand

and the corals, carefully hidden and immobile in their refuge. Move slowly, having already set aperture and exposure time. Approach the head of the turtle; when you get too close it will undoubtedly abandon its refuge quite lazily, enabling you to take two or three images. Avoid the classic image of your dive buddy straddling the shell of the turtle—they do not like it.

E

F

G

H

D

A. The surface of this coral relief appears excavated and molded by the force of the sea, the encrusting and per-forating organisms, and the growth of corals.

B. The snout of the hawksbill turtle (Eretmochelys imbricata) terminates in a very sharp beak. These turtles are not rare, and it is not unusual to observe them mating.

C. A fascinating image of a large brain coral block with a particu-larly rounded form. These hard corals owe their name to the sinuous reliefs of the coral walls.

D. A spheric brain coral lies on the sea bed.

E. Snappers, grunts, and small oceanic fish surround immobile corals.

F. A group of oriental sweetlips (Plecto-rynchus sp.) lingers under the vault of a cavity in the reef, waiting for twilight to venture forth in search of the benthic invertebrates on which they feed.

G. A close-up of the convolutions of brain coral. Apparently lifeless, by night these hills bloom as the polyps, closed by day to avoid too much intense raiding, expand.

H. Colonies of large acropora, with stocky finger-shaped branches, become the territory of chromis, which divide the labyrinth of branches among them according to their size, rank, and sex.

Kelso Reef

Kelso Reef, a couple of hours north from Townsville, is large, with a pronounced elongated form. In this part of the Great Barrier Reef, you don't find the long bands of huge elongated reef, drastically separating the open sea from shore areas, that characterize the area off Cairns. Here the coral constructions are more isolated, disconnected from

A

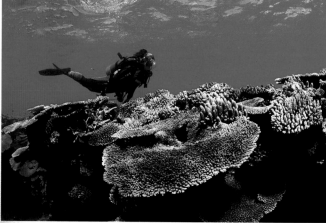

B

one another, forming an area of transition rather than a clear line of demarcation between sea and lagoon. The Kelso area is particularly interesting because it can be reached in a day by catamaran from the port of Townsville.

A floating fixed platform has been installed here as in other sectors of the Great Barrier Reef. The platform serves as base for the various activities planned for the excursionists. During a one-day visit to Kelso Reef you can dive, snorkel, and take trips on glass-bottomed boats. You can set out from the pontoon to about 10 dive sites in calm, not very deep waters, taking advantage of the shelter offered by the great main structure of Kelso Reef. Visibility is always quite good in this area because of the proximity of the open sea and the absence of a continuous barrier. The underwater excursions take place around small articulated reefs

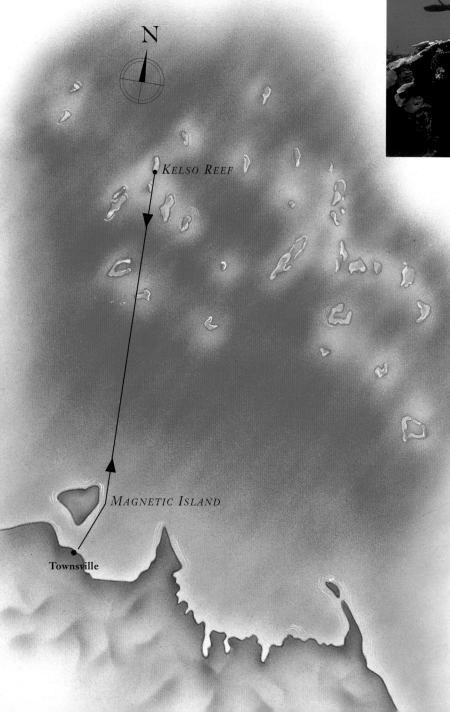

N

KELSO REEF

MAGNETIC ISLAND

Townsville

A. Fast boats carry divers to the numerous diving spots along Kelso Reef; all the dives are in calm, relatively shallow waters.

that rise from sandy sea beds from 65 or 33 feet (20 or 10 meters) almost to the surface. The coral life is varied and luxurious, and there is no shortage of barrier fish, giant clams, and small whitetip reef sharks. Daily cruises such as this one present an excellent opportunity for those who have traveled to Australia without intending to dedicate themselves to diving to at least take a look at these magnificent sea beds.

C

D

F

B. In sheltered waters, the platform-shaped acropora tend to colonize vast areas, exposing as much surface as possible to the sunlight. Light is indispensable for the life of the microalgae associated with the polyps.

C. The complex ramifications of this large acropora develop both horizontally and vertically.

D. The deer-horn acropora form an almost continuous belt along the areas of the barrier closest to the surface. At the base of these colonies you often find numerous branches, broken by the waves, that sometimes resume growing.

E. A very large giant clam (Tridacna gigas) opens its wide valves, revealing its fantastic brightly colored mantle.

F. The balance among the different species of the Great Barrier Reef is illustrated in this image, where the opened valve of a giant clam seems to try to resist the growth of the surrounding corals, which are forming a cage around the mollusc.

The Olgas

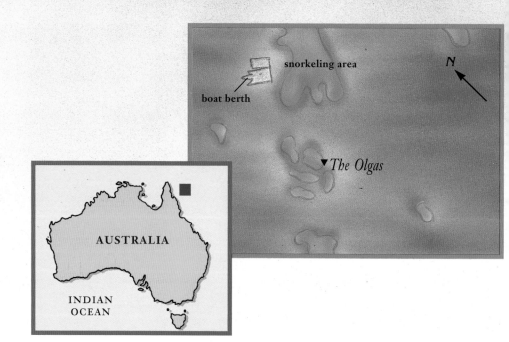

snorkeling area

boat berth

N

AUSTRALIA

INDIAN
OCEAN

The Olgas

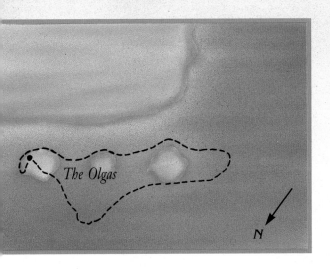

The Olgas

N

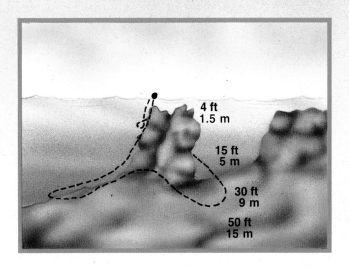

4 ft
1.5 m

15 ft
5 m

30 ft
9 m

50 ft
15 m

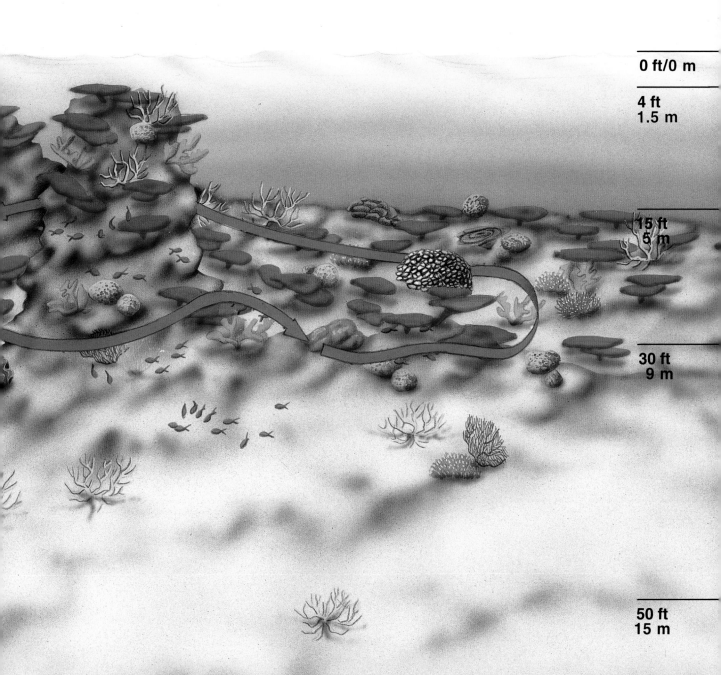

0 ft/0 m

4 ft
1.5 m

15 ft
5 m

30 ft
9 m

50 ft
15 m

The coral structure known as the Olgas is part of Kelso Reef, described in the previous itinerary. The dive at the Olgas, like the others on Kelso Reef, is relatively easy. The site presents little difficulty in terms of depth, orientation, or currents. It is very near the fixed platforms where the catamarans moor, just a few feet southeast.

The dive at the Olgas is quite similar to Two Buoys in many aspects; probably because the two sites are very close to one another. However, you immediately realize that the Olgas is richer and more varied. The morphology of the reef appears quite complex, consisting of a main, massive body with a series of bommies and secondary coral structures. The abundance of small barrier fish and the giant clams here and there among sand and coral is amazing. Soft corals, small yellow

A

B

A. Tabular, ramified, and massive formations coexist on a few square feet, dividing the territory according to habits that man only partially understands.

B. The entire coral area of the Olgas is very rich in different types of acropora, which mix and alternate over long stretches.

C

D

C. This coral pinnacle has been colonized by tabular acropora that grow in spiral formation along its perimeter to avoid obstructing the penetration of the sun.

D. A young grouper remains immobile, sheltered by the large acropora umbrella growing on top of a coral block. Seen from below, the structure of this colony reveals a complex tangle of branches that seem to support one another.

and red alcyonarians, and enormous bushes of sarcophyton grow here.

The fixed mooring for the platform tender is on top of a coral tower at about 45 feet (14 meters), which rises to several feet from the surface. The whole tower is very rich in different kinds of acropora. Descend the mooring rope to come face-to-face with the main body of the reef, a massive, elongated structure that ends in a plateau about 3 to 6 feet (1 to 2 meters) from the surface. The area is incredibly rich in live corals. It drops vertically to a softly inclined detrital slope at 15 or 20 feet (5 or 6 meters) that is covered with sporadic corals. This slope ends at the base of the coral tower where you began the dive, and at the base of two others, equally rich in acropora and other corals.

Between the second, less prominent relief and the more pronounced third one, a beautiful giant clam lives at the edge over a sharp drop to the sand at about 50 feet (15 meters). Proceed beyond both the main reefs and the base of the last tower and you find yourself in a very spacious area, very rich in coral fish, hard and soft corals, coral blocks, and crinoids. You may see turtles and whitetip reef sharks here, as well as dense schools of sergeant majors and isolated specimens of barramundi. Look carefully here for the enormous soft green sarcophyton corals and the large spectacular colonies of povona with dome-shaped apertures.

There are numerous giant clams in this area, but the largest of them lives under the boat mooring at 33 feet (10 meters). On the sand near this giant clam, massive and branching coral formations and some isolated branches of gorgonians grow.

PHOTOGRAPHY

Focus on the corals, using a wide-angle lens to capture the reef's richness in the clear waters. Try to avoid large scenes and concentrate on some of the large organisms found in these waters, such as the soft corals, the giant clams, or the enormous povona.

E. Giant clams are abundant among the corals of the Olgas; their brightly colored mantles stand out against the pale hues of the corals.

F. A cavity produced by the erosion of a coral block has been colonized by a sea anemone and a group of black and orange anemonefish or clownfish (Amphiprion melanopus).

G. Highly developed colonies of hard coral, extending over several square feet even though they only grow a few inches a year, are one of the best examples of the vital force of the entire barrier.

Two Buoys

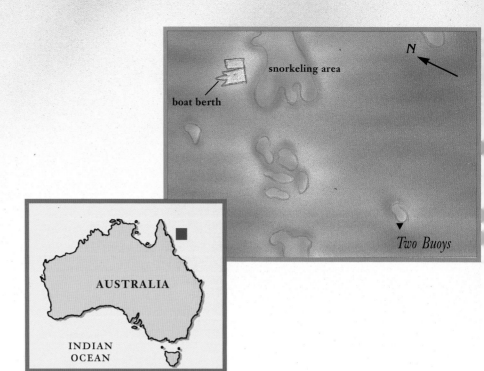

snorkeling area

boat berth

N

AUSTRALIA

INDIAN OCEAN

Two Buoys

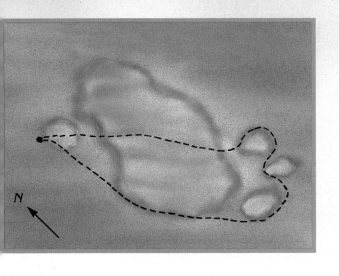

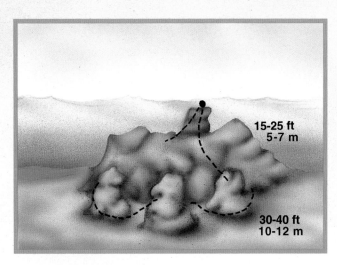

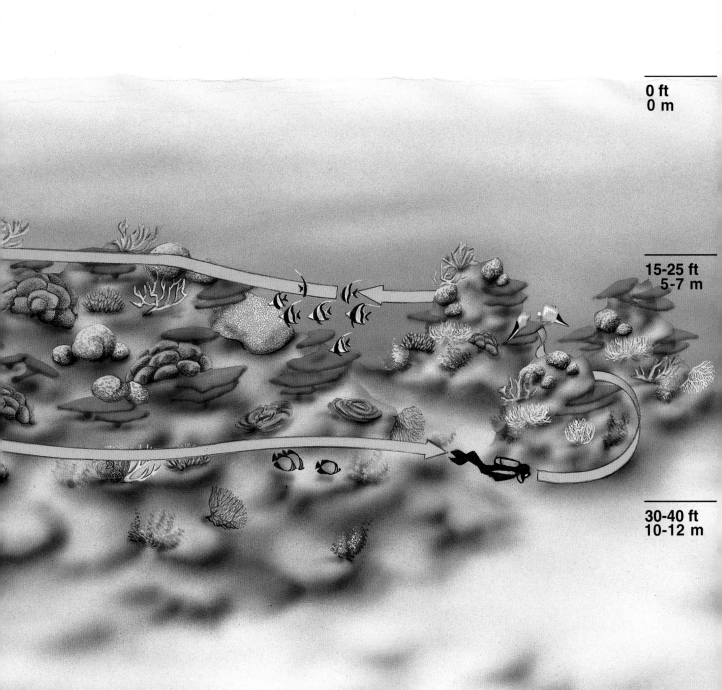

0 ft
0 m

15-25 ft
5-7 m

30-40 ft
10-12 m

15-25 ft
5-7 m

30-40 ft
10-12 m

This dive takes place on the sea bed of Kelso Reef, part of the central section of the Great Barrier Reef off Townsville. You can reach Kelso Reef on a day trip, without having to go on a multiday cruise. A large floating platform is anchored permanently near the reef; it serves as a base for the catamarans that shuttle between the site and the coast daily. An excursion usually includes two planned dives, one before and one after lunch, both near the base platform where the boat is moored. Two Buoys owes its name to the two buoys that indicate the mooring rope for the tender that transports the divers from the platform. You can clearly see the reef from the surface. It is a coral structure with an elliptical profile. The main axis measures about 165 feet (50 meters). A series of somewhat detached structures lies to the south. The mooring is fixed to the

A

B

A. Along Kelso Reef you often find rich formations of soft corals, whose bright colors stand out in the semidarkness.

B. This strange area, seemingly covered by stones, is really a large colony of hard corals (Povona sp.), whose polyps are grouped in small formations united by a common calcareous matrix.

C. These leaf-shaped corals cover the flattest areas of the reef, forming a uniform carpet that leads to the creation of large, shaded spaces very rich in fish and invertebrates who do not enjoy too much light.

D. Giant clams often attract divers, because of their size and the fact that they settle in the center of isolated coral formations.

C

D

top of a coral tower a little detached from the main body of Two Buoys. The dive mainly concentrates on the southern side of the reef. The entire structure is not very large. The main axis is not much longer than 165 feet (50 meters) and the width is little more than 100 feet (30 meters). The depth of the sea bed is very limited. In fact, you never descend deeper than 60 feet (18 meters). All this makes the dive very easy and suited to beginners.

You enter the water from the boat and swim toward the main body of the reef, above the sandy sea bed, which is about 55 feet (17 meters) below. When you approach the coral structure you are immediately astonished by the incredible quantity of coral blocks, one on top of the other, forming a living structure that does not leave as much as a square inch of naked rock. Flat or branching acropora, povona, montipora, porites, and goniopora make up a living castle of a bizarre and surprising architecture, favored by the quite clear waters and the bright light. Swim slowly to admire this scene, always keeping the coral wall to your left, moving southeast, until you see three pretty round coral reliefs, quite rich in barrier fish. At this point, where sand and coral meet, it is common to find turtles and small whitetip reef sharks. When you reach the area with these isolated formations, you usually have to face a current of varying intensity, from which you can easily find shelter behind the structures on the sea bed. After exploring the reef, you return to the boat by swimming above the main reef at a depth of between 15 and 25 feet (5 and 8 meters).

PHOTOGRAPHY

This dive offers many possibilities for the photographer. We recommend focusing on wide-angle photographs to show the richness of hard coral in this part of the sea. You may also choose to take portraits of coral fish, which are quite abundant and tame, accustomed to meeting divers. It is possible to get very colorful images, in spite of the generally monochrome character of the coral environment, by keeping a 50-mm macrophotography lens in the case.

E

F

G

E. A small gorgonian with white polyps stands out against the red of a sea fan.

F. The sea beds of Kelso Reef astonish divers with their incredible quantity of hard coral formations heaped on top of one another, creating a living structure that does not even leave a tiny space free.

G. A large leather coral (Sarcophyton sp.) projects from the sea bed with its typical plurilobed and sinuous form, reminiscent of brain coral.

A

A. The extremely well equipped fleet of yachts based in Cairns can meet the requirements of any diver, experienced or novice.

B. Crystal clear waters and currents rich in plankton are the main causes of the sometimes monumental dimensions reached by gorgonian sea fans in the Coral Sea.

B

Holmes Reef

Holmes Reef, like Flinders Reef, grows vertically from the abyssal depths of the Coral Sea and is surrounded by uncommonly clear waters. Here also, the dives are marked by the wealth of large, rich walls, such as the famous Abyss. The bommie walls have everything the Australian sea can offer in terms of benthic life and color. You can swim through dense schools of jacks, watch hammerhead sharks in the deep waters, and swim above enormous alcyonarians. In fact, while Holmes Reef is decidedly smaller than Flinders Reef, the features of the sea beds are more or less the same. Some tour operators organize shark-feeding dives at Holmes Reef, too.

There are a couple of easy and particularly beautiful dives here in shallow water over white sandy sea

Cairns

HOLMES REEF

Innisfail

Tully

N

C. Descending along one of the large walls of Holmes Reef, you can encounter every kind of benthic organism. Sponges, soft corals, hard corals, gorgonians, and tunicates cover the entire wall, animated by myriad fish and invertebrates.

beds interrupted by luxuriant and brightly colored coral islands. These simple dives are by no means less fascinating and spectacular than the deep dives. Holmes Reef is easily reached from Cairns, the regular departure point for cruise boats. Cruises to Holmes Reef are quite short because the reef is small. On the return trip, these cruises can include one or more days of diving in the Great Barrier Reef.

E

C

D

F

D. An extraordinary yellow soft coral; alcyonarians of this hue are rare elsewhere but quite common here. They capture all the light of the divers and reflect it in the surrounding water.

E. It is always an unforgettable experience to swim above a forest of gorgonians accompanied by hundreds of fish in continuous movement.

F. This large coral block, which rises isolated in the center of a coral platform, serves as landmark for a full exploration of the Barrier Reef in absolute safety.

The Cathedral

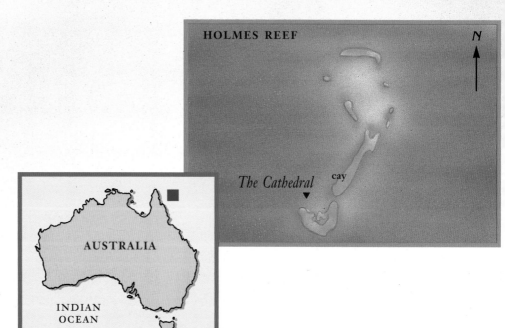

HOLMES REEF

N

The Cathedral

cay

AUSTRALIA

INDIAN OCEAN

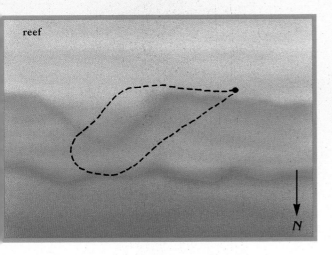

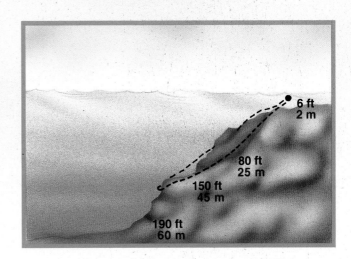

6 ft
2 m

80 ft
25 m

150 ft
45 m

190 ft
60 m

N

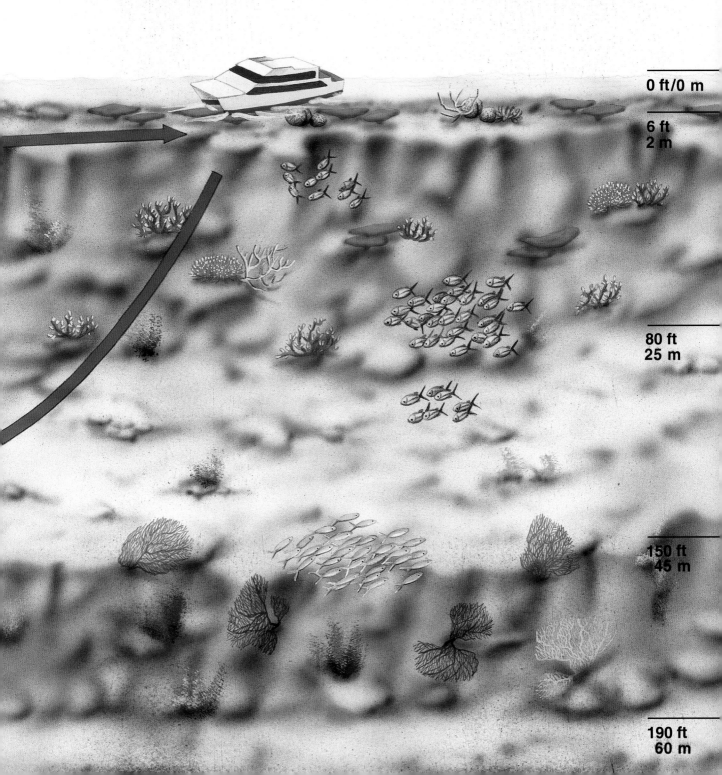

0 ft/0 m

6 ft
2 m

80 ft
25 m

150 ft
45 m

190 ft
60 m

The Cathedral is in the southern part of Holmes Reef, facing west, protected from the tide entering from the open sea. It includes ample reefs that descends to a ledge at about 100 feet (30 meters). From there it drops off sheer to between 150 and 200 feet (45 and 60 meters). There is a fixed mooring point, which provides a point of reference for the path followed during this dive. The boat is moored to a buoy fixed to the reef. In front of the boat, the coral barrier is clearly visible through the crystal clear water. The reef proceeds for 325 feet

B

C

D

A

(100 meters) to the right and then turns noticeably on itself to face the open sea. It goes much farther to the left, and that is the direction that you should swim. Following the mooring line, you reach the coral wall and cross it diagonally, keeping it to your right, while you continue your descent. You should reach the point where the wall meets the detrital slope at around 80 feet (25 meters). To find the point where the organisms are most beautiful and luxuriant, continue in this direction until the rock plunges deeper, reaching 100 feet (30 meters). The area

A. Due to the erosion of the corals and the force of the waves, some crevices penetrate deep into the reef, creating passages rich in fish, fascinating to explore.

B. Seen from the outside, the coral barrier seems to be a series of isolated formations, which are actually only the surfacing parts of an immense continuous formation that stretches as far as the eye can see.

C. The color contrasts visible from the surface become an irresistible invitation to divers. Boats are usually moored to fixed buoys in order not to damage the reef.

D. A hard coral with large leaves expands on the sea bed, developing its colonies in circular forms that guarantee full exposure to light for the polyps.

E. Coral blocks of the Favidae family can reach considerable sizes and create structures distinguished by the regular distribution of polyps, whose coral structures are raised and distinct from one another.

you are looking for is between the foot of the wall and the ledge below, at about 150 feet (45 meters). This area is very rich in giant gorgonians and alcyonarians. Beyond this point the sea bed drops once again, to more than 200 feet (60 meters), before it finally meets the sediment sea bed. The deep wall covered with gorgonians beckons, but it is better to resist this temptation and begin to ascend the reef wall, which you can follow up to 7 or 10 feet (2 or 3 meters) from the surface. Once you have reached a safe depth after this demanding dive, begin to return to the boat, this

time keeping the wall to your left. Don't forget to take a look at the deep fissures that cut into the reef: they are often full of groups of small trevally.

PHOTOGRAPHY

The pretty gorgonians and alcyonarians that rise vertically from the sea bed present easy and spectacular subjects. Taking care to compose the image and aiming the lens a little upward, it is possible to include the immense wall in the background with the surface and deep blue sea in one frame and get a dramatic image.

F. This coral formation, similar to a cooled lava flow, is animated by small Christmas tree worms (Spirobranchus giganteus), with typical tentacular crowns like tiny spruces.

G. The projecting parts of the reef walls are always colonized by gorgonian sea fans, which prosper in currents.

H. This yellow soft coral, seemingly lit from within, rises majestically from the sea bed, expanding its branches and polyps in a ray formation.

I. A large coral opens like a funnel, to the amazement of the diver in front of it.

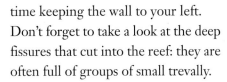

The Abyss

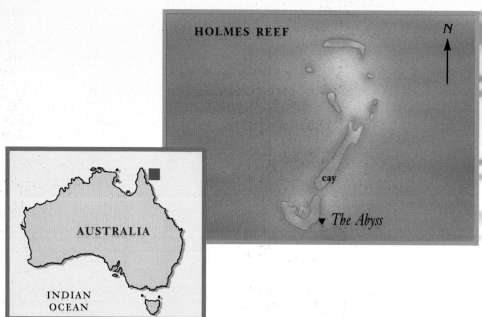

HOLMES REEF

N

cay

▼ The Abyss

AUSTRALIA

INDIAN
OCEAN

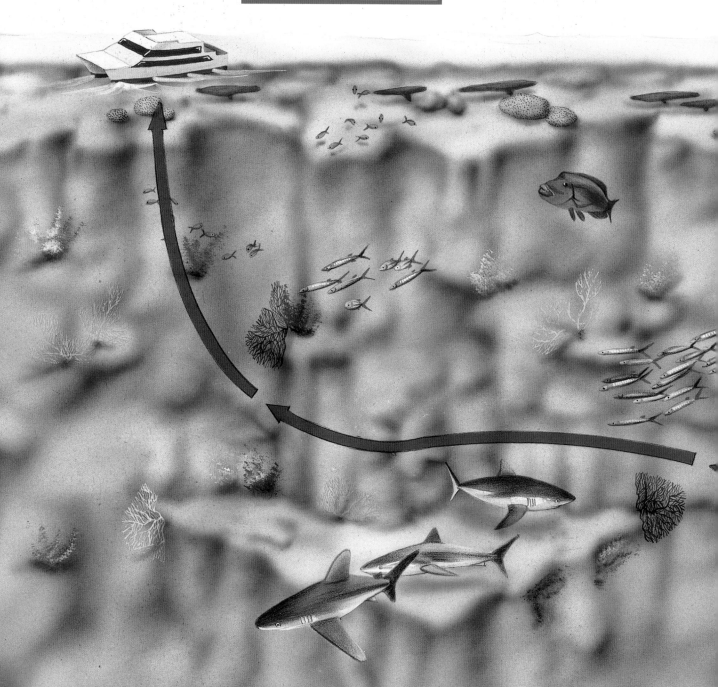

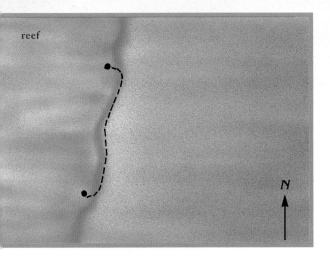

reef

N

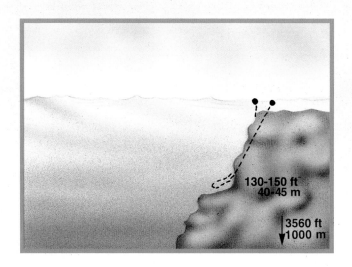

130-150 ft
40-45 m

3560 ft
1000 m

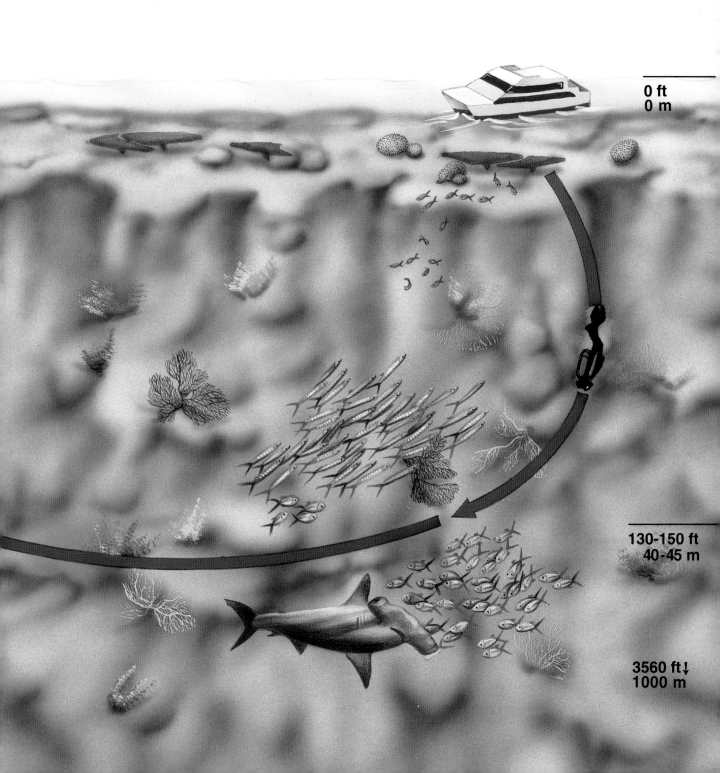

0 ft
0 m

130-150 ft
40-45 m

3560 ft↓
1000 m

A. The slender branches of a large gorgonian sea fan appear flimsy.

B. The clear water and abundance of large gorgonians suggest the use of wide-angle lenses for environmental images.

C. The incredible clarity of Coral Sea waters allows you to see everything from a considerable distance.

This is a favorite site among divers. In fact, Holmes Reef owes its deserved fame to the Abyss. It is in the southern area of Holmes Reef, on the side exposed to the open sea. The external wall drops to more than 1,640 feet (500 meters). It is, therefore, impossible to moor the boat and you must drift dive—the yacht follows the divers, waiting for them to surface. Sea conditions have to be excellent for drift dives. You cannot possibly approach the wall when waves are breaking against the reef and the wind is driving the boat toward it.

The dive at the Abyss follows the classical scheme of a drift dive. It is up to the skipper to determine the intensity and direction of the current, ensure that all divers are ready at the same time, and only then approach the reef for the few seconds necessary for the whole group to enter the water and begin moving in the planned direction. The divers must be ready to jump quickly into the water when they are told, immediately contact their buddies, and swim toward the wall, keeping an eye on the rest of the group. During a drift dive it is extremely

A

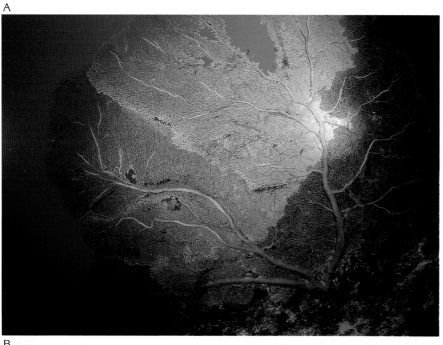

C

B

important that the group remain united from beginning to end, so that the boat can pick up everyone without difficulty. The incredible clarity of the waters of the Coral Sea helps with this. You can easily see your buddy and the majestic wall from quite a distance.

It is a good idea to descend to the planned depth immediately after entering the water and proceed from there, gradually reducing the depth, and eventually making a safety stop at 10 feet (3 meters) on the edge of the reef. You come across marvelous sights at all depths; the wall is equally rich at 33 feet (10 meters) and at 130 feet (40 meters), although you must go deeper to see the great oceanic predators.

The wall is rich in coral blocks and hard corals at depths from 3 to 50 feet (1 to 15 meters). Fascinating fissures with numerous schools of small fish open in the coral a few feet below the surface. At greater depths, the hard coral becomes more scarce, and you see enormous fans of gorgonians and alcyonarians as large as trees. You must not forget to keep an eye on the blue of the open sea for large oceanic species. The Abyss is one of the dive sites where you are most likely to meet large deep-sea sharks.

There is a pronounced horizontal ledge, almost a balcony, that projects toward the abyss at about 130 feet (40 meters). You find it by swimming along the wall, but it is hard to distinguish from the surface, and unless you can locate it by reference points on the reef, you may not be able to visit it. A large number of beautiful gray reef sharks usually gather here. In open water, at even greater depths, you may see the unmistakable outline of hammerhead sharks below you. The cruise yachts always visit this location, but, unfortunately, usually only toward the end or halfway through the dive, when it is absolutely unthinkable to descend so deep again.

PHOTOGRAPHY

The clear water and large number of enormous gorgonians and alcyonarians suggest the use of a very wide-angle lens to take environmental photographs. However, at the Abyss it is worthwhile to risk using a less extreme lens to try to get fascinating images of large fish, such as tuna and sharks, against the deep blue sea, using a flash.

D

E

F

G

F. As you descend along the wall, the hard corals are gradually replaced by gorgonians and soft corals, less dependent on the penetration of light and more dependent on the orientation of the substratum and the presence of currents.

G. At great depths, where the light is filtered, colonies of soft corals become larger and create rows of small colored trees.

D. A school of barracuda accompanies divers. This type of dive is typical of the Abyss, a reef that plunges into the blue, toward open sea.

E. This gorgonian sea fan has very sturdy branches that support other filtering organisms, including large black crinoids.

The Nonky

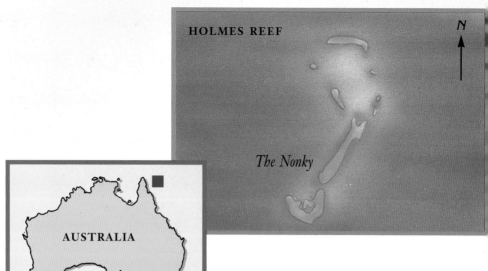

HOLMES REEF

N

The Nonky

AUSTRALIA

INDIAN
OCEAN

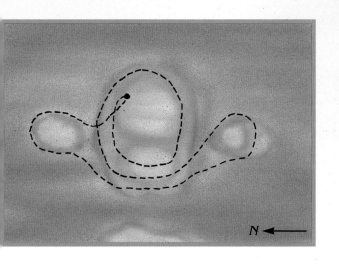

N

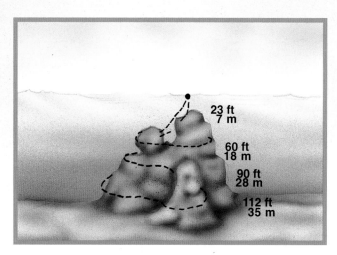

23 ft
7 m

60 ft
18 m

90 ft
28 m

112 ft
35 m

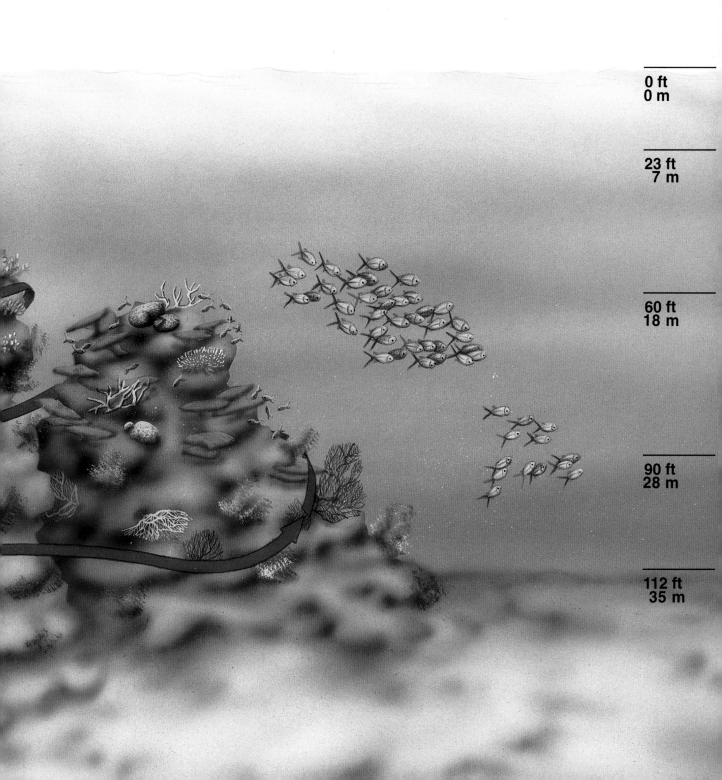

0 ft
0 m

23 ft
7 m

60 ft
18 m

90 ft
28 m

112 ft
35 m

A. At many points, the sea bed is formed of underwater reliefs surrounding a large bommie. In such places, the coral rapidly turns into rock that is equally rapidly colonized by different benthic organisms.

B. When completely expanded, the soft corals reveal their structure: increasingly slender branches on which polyps are arranged in clusters.

C. Jacks are just one of the many wonderful sights at Nonky Bommie.

D. Schools of jacks usually swim along the reef walls, carried by the dominant currents. Here they can find their prey, smaller fish and nektonic crustaceans.

E. The currents that flow into the reef crevices favor the gorgonians that grow on both walls, facing each other.

F. Deep crevices open along the coral towers, offering ideal growing conditions for large alcyonarians, such as this golden yellow one on the bottom of an underwater canyon.

G. In the blue of the surrounding water, far from direct light, bright gorgonians assume an unusually pale, almost lunar hue.

H. The sandy sea bed is scattered with residuals of dead corals, which form a suitable substratum for the settlement of brightly colored soft corals.

A
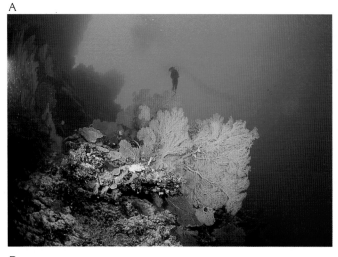

B

C

D

onky is a coral bommie that emerges from the sea bed at about 130 feet (40 meters) to about 23 feet (7 meters) from the surface. It is inside a large reef whose form resembles a question mark, protecting it from the southeastern winds. You are north of the dive called Amazing and not far from the sandy lagoon where shark feeding takes place. The fixed mooring place is on top of the large tower, at about 23 feet (7 meters).

We recommend circling the bommie after having reached the

E

planned maximum depth, gradually rising toward the surface. As soon as you enter the water, you realize that, in addition to the large coral tower below you, there are numerous underwater reliefs surrounding it. For this reason, it is advisable to dive no deeper than 130 feet (40 meters). Glide toward the sea bed along the walls of the large tower to reach the base of the rocks between 100 and 115 feet (30 and 35 meters). A number of more or less rounded forms project from here. Two of them, in particular, deserve mention: the first is north of the main tower and rises to 90 feet (28 meters); the second, much bigger, is on the opposite side and rises within 60 feet (18 meters) of the surface. The beauty of the enormous branches of alcyonarians and gorgonians that colonize their walls defies description. After having explored the two secondary reliefs, focus once more on the main one, aiming to arrive just under the boat on the western wall. Here, above a wall full of gorgonians, a deep and wide horizontal fissure full of sea organisms, from gorgonians to gigantic alcyonarians, opens at 70 feet (22 meters). The best colors and bold forms the coelenterates of the Australian seas offer are yet to come. Several feet above the fissure you see a deep incision in the tower, which is unbelievably rich in life, both fish and gorgonians. A magnificent golden yellow alcyonarian that soars from the bottom of the channel is the most amazing organism. Outside the fissure, which is 50 feet (15 meters) deep, in the direction of the plateau with its luxuriant coral growth, you may be able to swim among a dense school of jacks.

PHOTOGRAPHY

This is one of those dives for which you would like to have every lens available on the market, from the most extreme close-up to the widest of wide-angles, all at the same time. This would certainly be the worst mistake you could make here, however. Try not to let yourself be distracted by the exceptional abundance of subjects. Concentrate on something specific, such as the jacks or the alcyonarians, or even macrophotography. The best advice we can give is to concentrate on the beautiful vertical fissures full of gorgonians and alcyonarians.

F

G
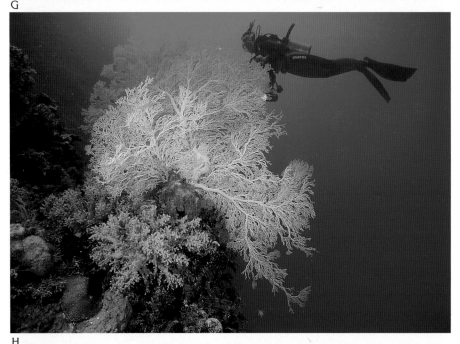

H

Amazing

AUSTRALIA

INDIAN
OCEAN

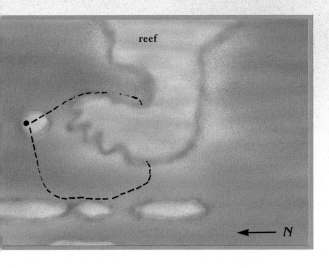

reef

N

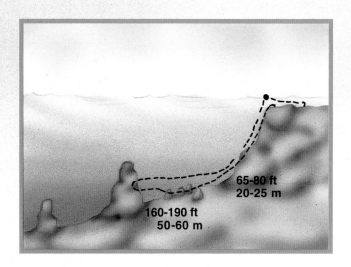

65-80 ft
20-25 m

160-190 ft
50-60 m

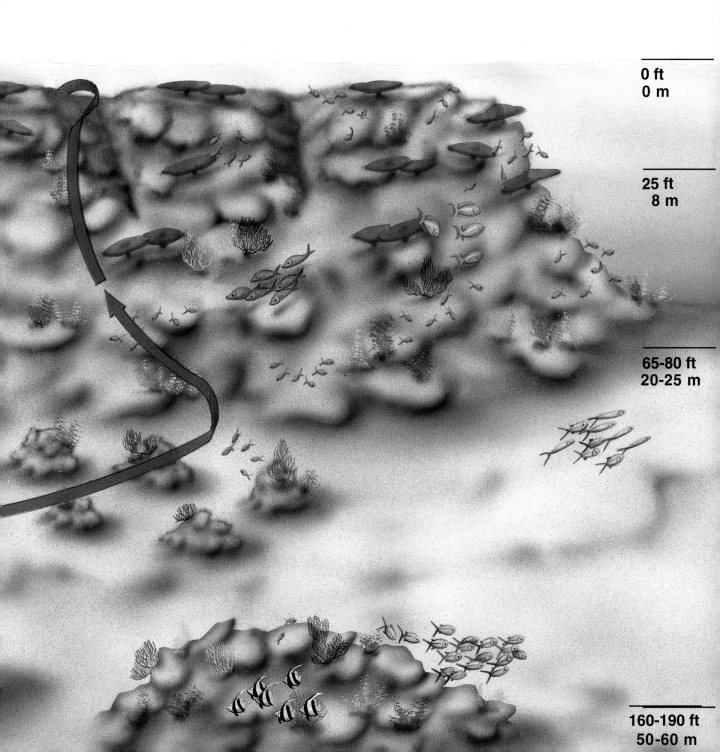

0 ft
0 m

25 ft
8 m

65-80 ft
20-25 m

160-190 ft
50-60 m

This dive takes place on the western side of the northern section of Holmes Reef, sheltered from the dominant south-eastern winds. It begins from a calm pleasant mooring point. The coral barrier almost touches the surface and then drops rapidly to great depths just below the stern of the boat. The mooring point is fixed to a coral tower not far from the reef. At Amazing, the routes focus on two areas completely different from one another in terms of morphology and depth. In one area you explore a series of successive ledges that lead

C

Enter the water from the stern and immediately let yourself descend in the clear water. The white sand slopes steeply to great depths below. The first things you see are the great rock masses projecting from the sand ahead. Spend some time exploring these splendid buttresses, which plunge in successive leaps from a minimum of 115 feet (35 meters) to unreachable depths.

The reef is densely populated by large branches of gorgonians, alcyonarians, and sponges. We advise against going below 130 feet (40 meters); your effort will not be

A

D

B

to very great depths, while in the other you focus on the relatively shallow walls of the main reef. The main reef itself consists of a series of canyons and tunnels that, crossing the wall, lead to the inside of lagoons with sandy sea beds surrounded by corals. The boat moors to a small bommie that ranges from 62 to 25 feet (19 to 8 meters). The main reef is clearly visible to the east, while the coral precipice is under the stern of the boat, to the west, provided that the dominant wind is from the southeast.

rewarded by any sensational sights. Between the tallest rock and the one whose peak reaches 130 feet (40 meters) there is a very beautiful fissure that deserves a visit. A beautiful composition of alcyonarians, sponges, and gorgonians stands out against the deep blue sea. After spending time at those depths, ascend along the sand, somewhat obliquely toward the right. At around 100 feet (30 meters) there is a series of isolated coral reefs, where a number of beautiful, intense red alcyonarians grow. Keeping a careful

A and I. The variety of forms that hard corals can assume compensates for their almost general lack of color. Soft corals, however, are extremely colorful but have typical arborescent forms with polyps gathered in clusters.

B. A stretch of tabular acropora grows on the upper part of these reefs, sheltered from the dominant winds and surrounded by clear waters.

C. At about 33 feet (10 meters) the reef has deep channels, some of which turn into tunnels leading to the interior of lagoons protected by the barrier.

D. The somewhat ruffled surface of the sea does not reduce the transparency of the water. In fact, the sediments are found too deep for the waves to suspend them.

E. A hard coral with a very ramified and intricate colony grows isolated on a rocky base, surrounded by sand. These formations attract many species of fish, especially chromis.

F. A green turtle (Chelonia mydas) swims just above the sea bed in search of the seaweed it usually feeds on.

G. The edge of a ledge looking to greater depths is concealed by these large gorgonians, particularly developed and numerous from the current that rises from the bottom.

H. These particular gorgonians form many sea fans along the main branches until the entire colony resembles a tangled bush.

E

F

G

H

check on your time and depth, gradually ascend a little toward the base of the reef wall, which meets the sand at about 65 feet (20 meters).

Stop at around 33 feet (10 meters), once you have reached the wall, where deep channels furrow the reef. Some of them become tunnels that, after a short stretch, lead to the inside of small lagoons beyond the barrier. At this point you are quite near the surface and can return to the boat by swimming around the main structure.

I

PHOTOGRAPHY

You can choose between two different types of image during this dive: colorful pictures of alcyonarians and gorgonians at great depths, and pictures from inside the coral grottos, against the natural light, without a flash. Look for the reflection of the corals on the water's surface, which is exquisite, because of the exceptional visibility and intense reflection of light off the white sand on the sea bed.

Flinders, Dart, and Myrmidon Reefs

Flinders Reef is a large reef lost in the immensity of the Coral Sea. Hundreds of miles off the Australian continent and the Great Barrier Reef, a formidable coral block tower rises from the sea floor from a depth of more than 3,280 feet (1,000 meters), at some points ending just a few inches from the surface. This enormous tower is some dozens of miles in diameter. An elliptic and discontinuous coral belt surrounds a lagoon with a sandy sea bed of about 200 feet (60 meters).

The impressive walls of the tower drop vertically to the ocean sea bed beyond the barrier. South Flinders, Dart Reef, and Herald Surprise are minor structures that rise near the larger Flinders Reef. This is usually the destination of the long cruises, and is probably the area where the sea of Queensland offers the most to divers. Immense, perpendicular walls that look into the abyss and bommies unbelievably rich in gigantic alcyonarians and gorgonians are the two types of dive site characteristic of this area. The crystal clear water, which guarantees uncommon visibility, is also a constant here.

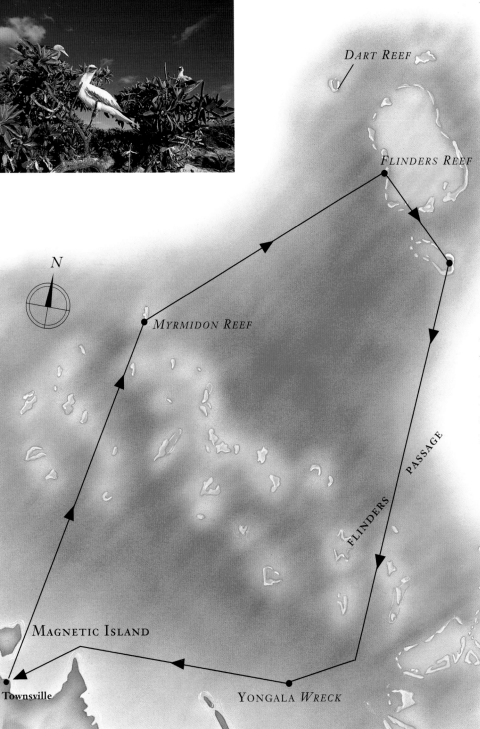

DART REEF

FLINDERS REEF

N

MYRMIDON REEF

FLINDERS PASSAGE

MAGNETIC ISLAND

Townsville

YONGALA WRECK

A. A dark mass can be distinguished clearly in the limpid water. It is a growing coral block that, in hundreds of years, may become a small island lined with white sand, like the one in the background.

B. In an environment such as that of the Great Barrier Reef, dominated by the sea, it is always amazing to discover that some islands have typical inland landscapes with trees and birds.

C. When diving at Flinders Reef, you find yourself suspended in the water alongside enormous gorgonian sea fans that sometimes reach a width of 16 feet (5 meters).

D. The vault of a tunnel frames a gorgonian that projects into the blue.

E. Soft corals can reach considerable sizes that emphasize the beauty of their translucent colors.

F. It is not unusual to come across turtles in these waters, where prey is abundant and there are numerous sheltered, quiet areas to lay their eggs.

G. Thanks to the transparency of the waters, you can see the abundance of underwater life and how deep areas alternate with shallow ones.

C

D

E

F

While many of the dives you may choose at Flinders Reef and its surrounding reefs are known and often repeated, there is an infinite stretch of completely unexplored outer walls and bommies inside the great lagoon. This enables some operators to offer those participating in diving charters a splendid combination of safe and tested dives with the thrill of exploring completely virgin sea beds. Being the first person to swim in these waters makes a cruise here a truly unique experience.

At Flinders Reef, you can expect to glide suspended along impressive,

G

endless walls and to swim past gorgonians 15 feet (5 meters) wide and yellow and red alcyonarians 6 feet (2 meters) tall.

Along with Flinders Reef, you will dive on two of the most spectacular sites of the Great Barrier Reef: Myrmidon Reef and the *Yongala* wreck. Myrmidon Reef offers a combination of the rich coral block growth of the Great Barrier Reef and the incredible visibility of the Coral Sea. The *Yongala* wreck is a beautiful passenger ship, unbelievably rich in fish, sunk off Cape Bowling Green.

Fan Fun, Flinders Reef

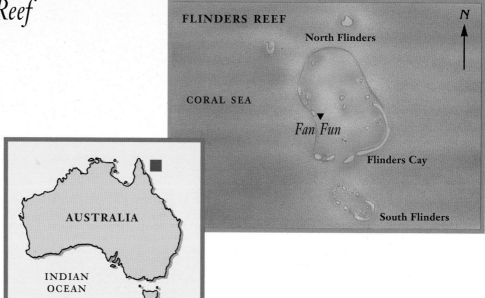

FLINDERS REEF
North Flinders
CORAL SEA
Fan Fun
Flinders Cay
South Flinders
N

AUSTRALIA
INDIAN OCEAN

0 ft
0 m

9 ft
3 m

15 ft
5 m

30-50 ft
10-15 m

60 ft
18 m

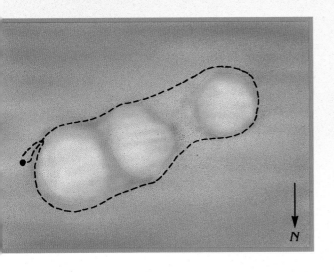

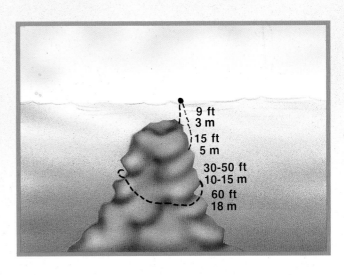

9 ft
3 m

15 ft
5 m

30-50 ft
10-15 m

60 ft
18 m

an Fun dive site is along the walls of two bommies that come up from the sea bed at about 165 feet (50 meters). The site is the southern extremity of Mid Reef, a coral buttress facing the abyss on the western edge of Flinders Reef perimeter.

The two bommie tops rise to 10 and 15 feet (3 and 5 meters) and are clearly visible from the surface. The boat usually moors so that the stern is close to the top of the larger bommie.

As soon as you enter the water, you see that the two coral forma-

B

tions are united by a common base that descends from 65 to 165 feet (20 to 50 meters). Our advice is to choose 65 feet (20 meters) as your maximum depth, so you can make a long and pleasant dive, circling the walls of the two underwater towers in their entirety.

The distinguishing feature of this stretch of sea bed is the large number of huge gorgonian branches, which adorn spectacular grottos and fissures opening in the coral rock. Start swimming, keeping the wall of the larger bommie to your right. After a short while, you find yourself

A
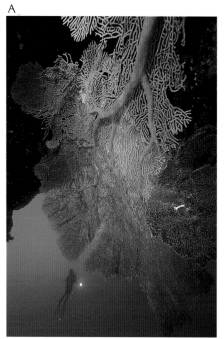

C

A. The large towers at Fan Fun are interrupted by deep crevices. Inside, you find a large number of gorgonian sea fans that belong to different species and can therefore grow close to one another.

B. Balancing on a sea bed looking into the abyss, this coral block seems to challenge gravity, entrusting its mass to a tiny calcareous disc.

C. In the tunnels that open among the bommies there is little space left between one colony of organisms and the next. Avoid exploring the interior —you risk destroying specimens many decades old.

D. The orientation of the gorgonian sea fans depends on the direction of the currents. Inside crevices, therefore, you find gorgonians that grow upward and downward.

D

in the saddle between the two bommies. Cross it, swimming toward the smaller bommie. Here, at exactly 65 feet (20 meters), is a tunnel 15 or 20 feet (5 or 6 meters) long, lined with beautiful corals of a subtle violet color. Observe them from the outside; a diver in there would probably have the same effect as a bull in a china shop.

Continue beyond the corner of the tower until you find one of the most gorgeous and photogenic points of the entire dive. At about 55 feet (17 meters), there is a wide grotto embellished with large branches of yellow gorgonians. Having left the grotto, cross the saddle once more and cruise the buttresses of the main tower. Just a little farther around the tower, there is another beautiful grotto. Then, at 65 feet (20 meters), the flat sea bed displays splendid branches of gorgonians with tips embellished by numerous black crinoids. Return to the wall and continue circling, still keeping the wall to your right, and rising a little. Between 33 and 50 feet of depth (10 and 15 meters), there is a splendid horizontal fissure practically packed with gorgonians. Face the interior, being careful not to touch the organ-isms, to find the group of wonderful batfish who live here. After visiting this fissure, rise to the top of the shallow, where many wonderful yellow and green soft corals grow.

PHOTOGRAPHY

The name of this dive suggests the main subject of your photographs. Use the widest of your wide-angles and, if possible, two flashes to obtain a uniform and soft lighting of the large golden yellow branches. Expose your photographs for natural light in order to get a pleasant and realistic blue background. Take great care not to overexpose the foreground with a direct flash too close to the subject.

E. Swimming around the coral towers of Fan Fun, you see crevices at regular intervals, each concealing large gorgonians.

F. To the diver watching them, these gorgonian sea fans seem to be superimposed. In fact, there is enough space between one colony and the next for currents to pass.

G. The most exposed walls of the coral tower are studded with large, pink-orange gorgonians.

H. The farthest points of the reef are an ideal habitat for all filtering organisms, which feed on particles brought by the currents.

Softwood Forest, Flinders Reef

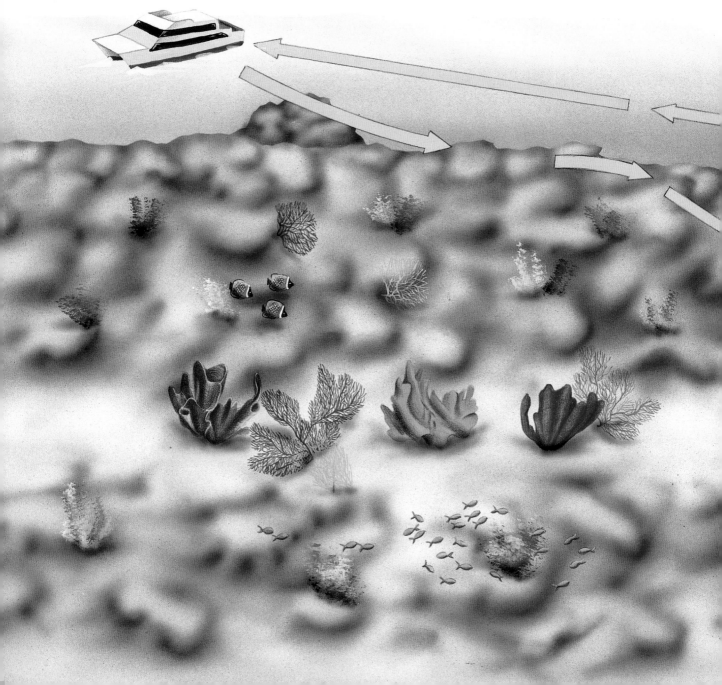

AUSTRALIA

INDIAN
OCEAN

FLINDERS REEF

North Flinders

N

CORAL SEA

Softwood Forest

Flinders Cay

South Flinders

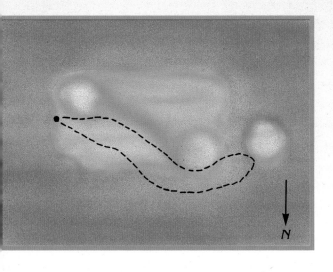

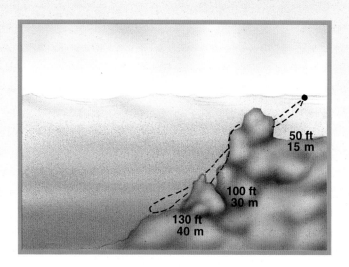

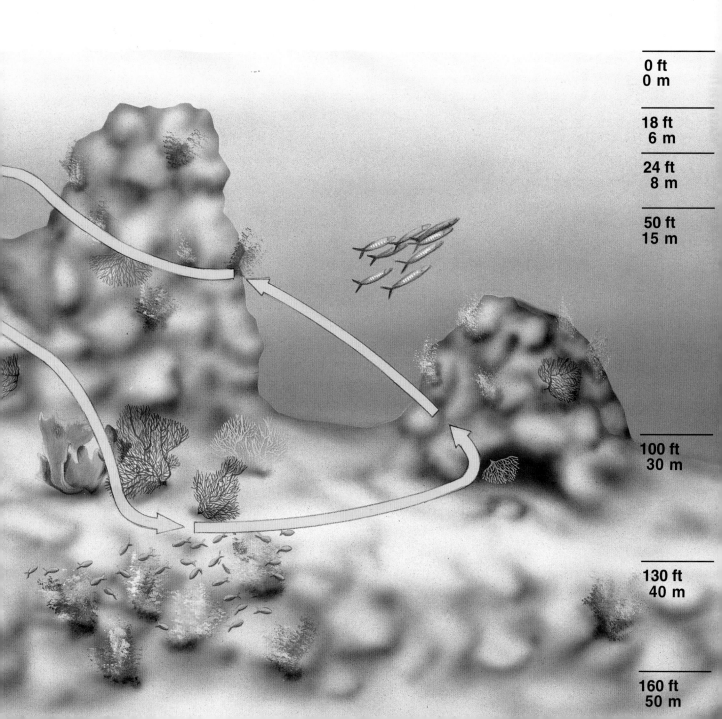

0 ft
0 m

18 ft
6 m

24 ft
8 m

50 ft
15 m

100 ft
30 m

130 ft
40 m

160 ft
50 m

Softwood Forest is a large coral bommie in the internal lagoon of Flinders Reef. It lies in the southwestern part of the large lagoon, a few miles from the slope that leads directly to the deep Coral Sea. It is clearly visible on the nautical chart as a small, elongated shoal that reaches about 25 feet (8 meters) and is surrounded by sea beds deeper than 200 feet (60 meters).

There is a fixed mooring place, and the boat's stern sits just above the southern end of the shallow. You can see the entire shallow as soon as you enter the water, thanks to the marvelous visibility. You can even glimpse the sandy sea bed 200 feet (60 meters) below your flippers.

There are two round elevations on the flat top of the enormous tower. The one nearest you goes from 33 or 40 feet (10 or 12 meters) to 25 feet (8 meters), and the smaller one reaches 20 feet (6 meters). Swim along the plateau to the second elevation. At its base on the inside, you find a channel that cuts into the corals. Enter this structure, protected from the strong currents that sometimes sweep the plateau, and follow it several feet, until it leads you to a splendid wall. Stop a moment to observe your surroundings; you are at about 65 feet (20 meters). The wall is covered by a luxuriant growth of wonderful medium-sized alcyonarians and small branches of gorgonians. The wall ends below in a sandy slope that drops from 100 to 130 feet (30 to 40 meters), where a second edge faces a sheer drop down to the sand more than 165 feet (50 meters) below.

A. The large coral towers that rise from the deep sandy plain are perforated by crevices and small grottos, whose entrances are only partially blocked by gorgonian sea fans.

B. The arborescent colonies of large dendroneftids, the most typical soft corals, always seem to grow at a certain distance from one another. It is not yet known if this phenomenon is casual or related to a particular requirement of these animals.

A

B

C

D

C. These enormous golden yellow alcyonarians grow in places where the light is very filtered, at depths that border on the maximum permitted by sports diving regulations.

D. Gorgonians that grow close to sandy sea beds often assume a candelabra shape with ramifications that are stocky and spongy in appearance when the polyps are completely expanded.

On the first strip of sand, between 100 and 130 feet (30 and 40 meters), there are splendid isolated branches of enormous sea fans and some beautiful examples of very large alcyonarians. To your left—with your back to the channel you just exited—you see a second shallow that ascends from about 115 to 65 feet (35 to 20 meters). Choose from the possible routes according to your level of experience and the intensity of the current. The simplest route involves a complete round of the shallow at depths between 65 and 80 feet (20 and 25 meters), at one point reaching a small isolated shallow with a grotto full of sea fans. You may also descend in the direction of the channel and go a bit deeper to the splendid sea fans on the sand; or even to the second edge, where you find a group of exceptionally large bright red and yellow alcyonarians.

PHOTOGRAPHY

Softwood Forest is the perfect location for wide-angle photography: 15 mm, 16 mm in the case, the Nikonos RS with its famous 13 mm lens. Who knows? Someone may even invent an even wider lens after diving these waters! The water at Softwood is incredibly transparent, so you can shoot wonderful images of the abundant and brightly colored benthic life that populates this sea bed.

Be careful: get as close as possible to your subject, expose for natural light, and use a couple of flashes placed far from one another to get even lighting. The enormous organisms are beautiful, but particularly hard to photograph.

E

F

E. An alcyonarian emerges from the sea bed with completely open polyps. Soft corals alternate periods with closed polyps and periods with polyps completely extended, open, and active.

F. Softwood Forest is perfect for wide-angle shots. This requires a good mastery of the camera and a careful balancing of environmental and artificial light.

G. A solitary tropical sea plume stands out against the sea bed, projecting its fleshy part, which it attaches to the sea bed. In spite of its appearance, this is a colonial organism formed by hundreds of polyps.

G

Midnite Reef, Flinders Reef

FLINDERS REEF

N

North Flinders

CORAL SEA

Midnite Reef

Flinders Cay

South Flinders

AUSTRALIA

INDIAN
OCEAN

0 ft
0 m

15 ft
5 m

80 ft
25 m

130 ft
40 m

160 ft
50 m

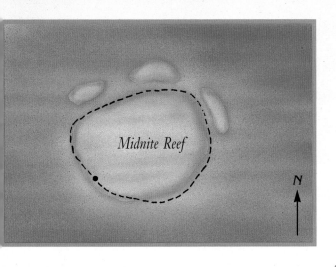

Midnite Reef

N

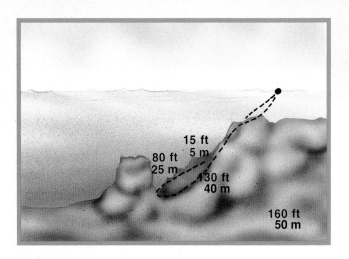

15 ft
5 m
80 ft
25 m
130 ft
40 m
160 ft
50 m

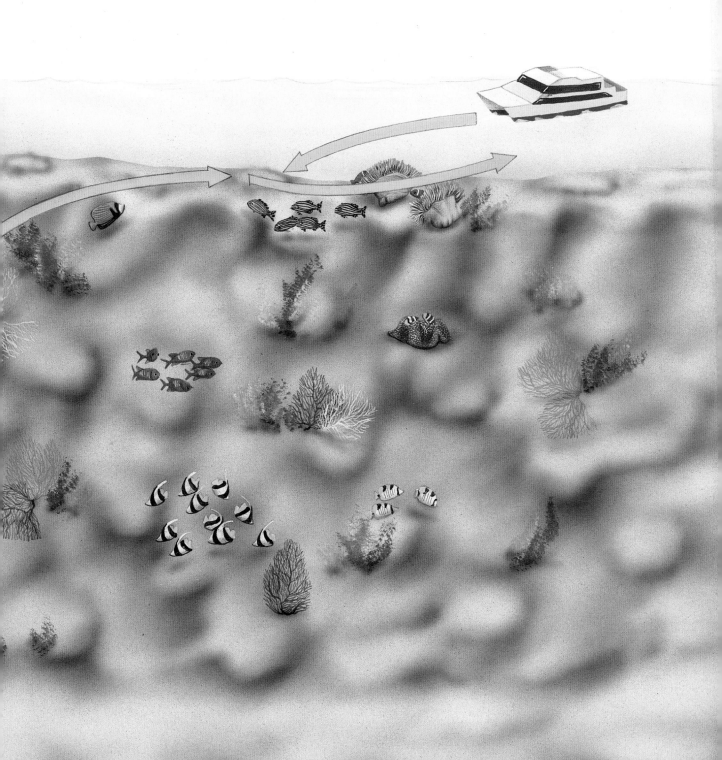

This spectacular bommie was recently discovered in the southwestern part of Flinders Lagoon. From the south, this reef looks like a large, thickset tower that ascends from about 165 to 23 feet (50 to 7 meters). A fixed mooring place is usually not used; the tour operators prefer to drop anchor on the sand at about 165 feet (50 meters). Mooring is reliable up to 50 knots of southeastern wind, which is dominant in this area.

The top of the bommie is home to a large variety of luxuriant hard and soft coral formations. The depth

C

A

D

B

on the plateau varies from 23 to 50 feet (7 to 15 meters). The entire area is particularly good for easy, beautiful night dives, made even more fascinating by numerous crayfish, octopuses, and moray eels. However, the part of the sea bed that makes this location one of the world's most beautiful is reserved for experienced divers. The walls here drop vertically to the surrounding sea bed, which varies between 130 and 165 feet (40 and 50 meters). Between 80 and 100 feet (25 and 30 meters) you find a great abundance of gorgonians, alcyonarians, crinoids, and corals. The open

waters are very rich in oceanic species, including sharks. You must follow a specific route to find the most interesting areas. The stern of the boat is on the southern side of the shallow because of the predominant southeastern wind. You must cross the plateau by swimming northeast. Stay above the edge of the wall facing northwest until you see a large elongated rock detached from the bommie's main body. Enter the channel, keeping the bommie wall on your left. You are at a depth of about 100 feet (30 meters). The canal is magnificent, full of large gorgonians and

A. Some canyons are difficult to cross because of the luxuriant growth of alcyonarians and gorgonians. To swim through these stretches of sea bed requires constant control of your movement to avoid damaging the organisms.

B. In some areas the Coral Sea could be renamed Fan Sea in honor of the abundance and profusion of gorgonian sea fans.

brightly colored alcyonarians; it is inhabited by a large quantity of fish, including a school of large blue surgeonfish.

At the end of the canal, you arrive at a saddle between the main shallow and a large monolith, the top of which is at 80 feet (25 meters) and the bottom at more than 165 feet (50 meters), on the side farthest from the large bommie. The saddle is a true underwater paradise. Alcyonarians of matchless beauty and size, sea fans, and large quantities of anthias thrive here. It is a place and sensation that you will never forget.

You have by now reached 130 feet (40 meters) and it is time to ascend. Turn your back to the small bommie and rise along the reef's vertical northern wall to the edge at about 50 feet (15 meters). Cross the plateau and return to the boat for the safety stop.

PHOTOGRAPHY

Forget macrophotography! Save it for the night dive. This shallow is so beautiful that it has to be shot with a wide-angle lens. The incredibly clear water makes everything easier. Descend to a beautiful spot with your camera, choose your subject carefully, and avoid being distracted by the richness of the organisms around you. Remember always to point the lens upward to recover the environmental light, which is somewhat scarce between 100 and 165 feet (30 and 40 meters), especially with the large bodies of the shallows above.

C. The arrangement of these large gorgonian sea fans seems to have been planned by an expert landscape gardener.

D. Where conditions are ideal, small alcyonarians form dense, colorful forests that oscillate under the force of the current.

E. On terraces that slope softly toward deep waters, colonies of tabular acropora, which grow in such a way so as not to shade one another, become more abundant.

F. In the waters near the surface, more illuminated and with greater current, coral blocks are abundant and luxuriant, especially massive forms such as brain corals.

G. A group of alcyonarians has colonized a small ledge in the vertical development of this coral tower, which is as tall as a 12-story building.

H. Descending along the reef walls, you discover that the life forms are also abundant at greater depths, where soft corals always play the main role.

Watanabe Bommie, Flinders Reef

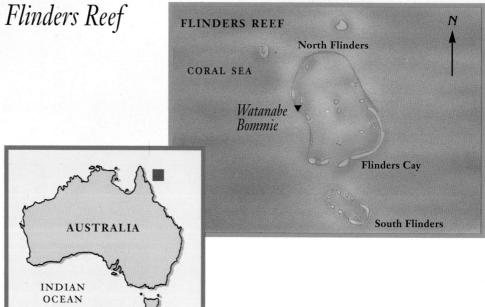

FLINDERS REEF

CORAL SEA

North Flinders

Watanabe Bommie ▼

Flinders Cay

South Flinders

N

AUSTRALIA

INDIAN OCEAN

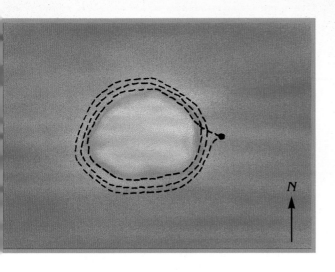

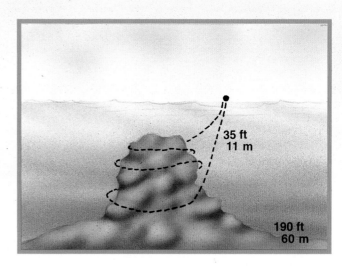

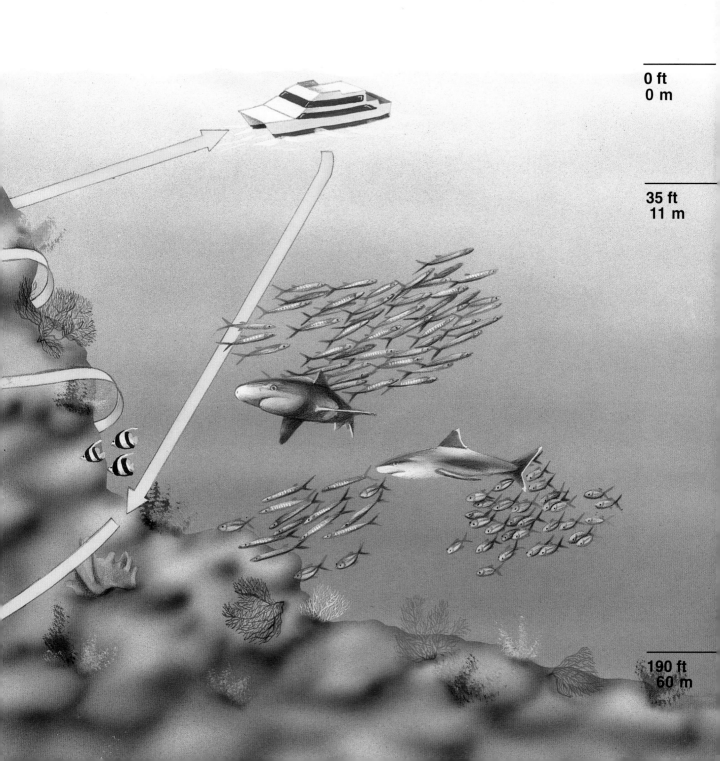

0 ft
0 m

35 ft
11 m

190 ft
60 m

A. On these sea beds there is an incredible show performed by nature: corals of an infinite variety of species, forms, and colors cover the reef.

B. Large colonies of benthic invertebrates dominate the underwater passage.

C. You often come across schools of jacks in these areas. They tend to remain in specific areas, enabling the diver to plan an encounter.

D. A large coral formation seems to catch fire, reflecting the light like a mirror.

E. The profile of the coral tower is marked by an almost continuous succession of soft corals and gorgonian sea fans.

F. Gorgonians and alcyonarians alternate regularly on each dive; it is hard to tire of sights like these.

G. These gorgonians, whose isolated branches converge in a single, short central axis, grow on sea beds swept by currents.

H. A black crinoid, its arms completely extended, stands out against the gorgonian sea fan it has chosen as a place of rest.

A

B

C

D

This coral pinnacle rises from the sandy sea floor at 200 feet (60 meters) to only 35 feet (11 meters) from the surface. You are in the center of the western part of Flinders Reef, near the point where the lagoon meets the immense wall that drops perpendicularly to the great depths of the oceanic sea bed.

The yachts usually drop anchor on the Watanabe sea bed around the base of the large tower, so the stern of the vessel is just over it. The boat usually remains anchored long enough to make several dives.

The profile of the dive plan does not look demanding. In fact, it is sufficient to descend to the desired depth and then rise in a circular path around the coral peak. However, do not underestimate the great depths surrounding the walls and the almost constant presence of very strong currents. When you plan the dive and choose the maximum depth, you must consider the current and the fact that you are sure to follow the schools of fish into open water, exerting yourself even more, which is hard on your air consumption. So pay attention! With a clear plan in mind, enter the water and begin descending the coral walls. Go to at least 100 feet (30 meters), where a beautiful grotto, full of fish, opens on the western side. Below the grotto the walls continue their vertical drop to about 150 feet (45 meters), where they begin a gentler slope to the sand at 200 feet (60 meters). The deeper areas are full of large gorgonians and alcyonarians. However, there is no need to descend to great depths—more or less the same organisms are found at less demanding depths. Nearer the surface you may experience the thrill of swimming through dense schools of barracuda and jacks, completely accustomed to the presence of divers. It is not uncommon to come across gray sharks in these areas. If you have planned a deep dive, you should not forget to leave enough time and air to be able to remain some minutes in the areas closer to the surface.

F

Try not to let yourself be carried away, taking one picture after the other without paying attention to the framing—a very serious error. The fish stay where they are; they don't escape, they just move away a little. Breathe slowly and cautiously so as not to scare them with the bubbles, and approach them by swimming slowly against the current. Then compose the image carefully and take one photograph before the school, disturbed by your presence, scatters. You have to start the procedure over for the next picture.

E

G

PHOTOGRAPHY

At Watanabe you will probably concentrate on the schools of fish. Equip yourself with an average wide-angle lens and one or two flashes. Evaluate the exposure required by the environmental light and adjust the lens aperture, using the lamps just to lighten and reduce the dominant blue, before you take pictures. Having completed these preparations very carefully, you can start shooting without having to worry about the technical aspects anymore.

H

Rock Arch, Flinders Reef

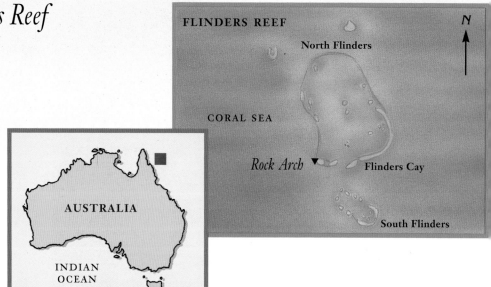

FLINDERS REEF

North Flinders

CORAL SEA

Rock Arch ▼   Flinders Cay

South Flinders

N

AUSTRALIA

INDIAN
OCEAN

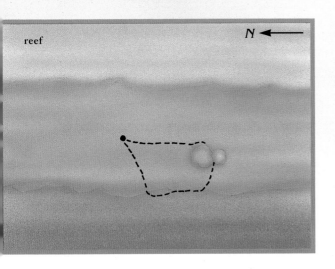

reef

N ←

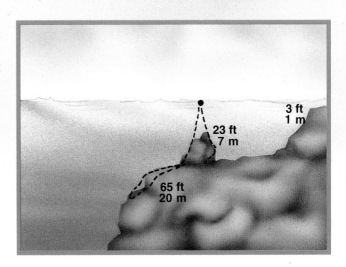

3 ft
1 m

23 ft
7 m

65 ft
20 m

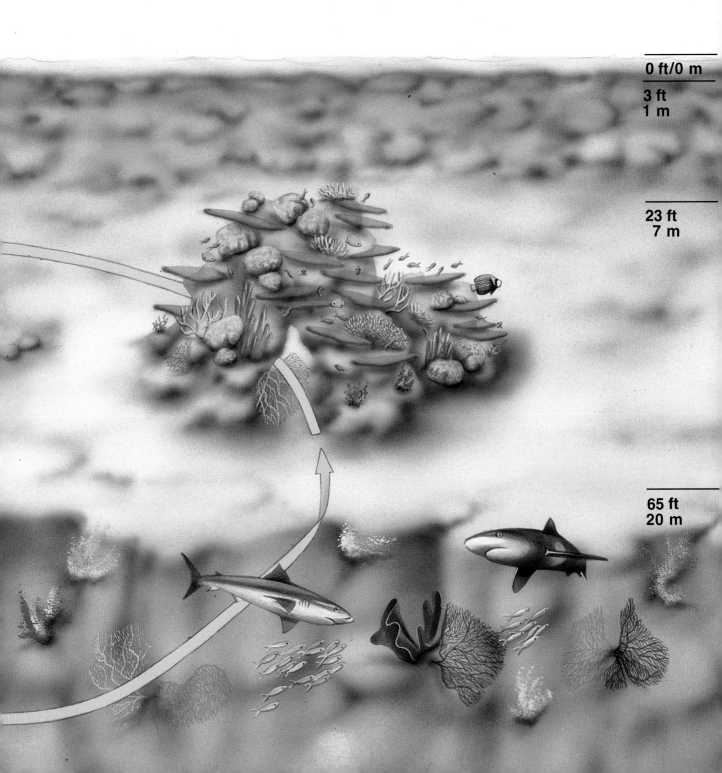

0 ft/0 m

3 ft
1 m

23 ft
7 m

65 ft
20 m

A. Supported by branches that are inches in diameter, this gorgonian forms an ample fan of several laminar expansions that, superimposed on one another, look like a continuous structure.

B. The hedge of the reefs that almost reach the surface are an ideal environment for long explorations suited to beginners or to photographers in search of new subjects without the restrictions associated with more demanding dive spots.

A

This dive site is at the south-western extremity of Flinders Reef. The mooring is on an isolated coral bommie in the coral barrier in a sandy bay with a steep slope. Beyond the sand, just north and south of this area, you see a formi-dable underwater wall facing northwest. Rock Arch can be good for a beginner who limits himself to exploring the reef buttresses, which reach almost to the surface. It can also be very demanding even for expert divers, who descend along the impressive wall that drops to levels well below 325 feet

B

D

C

(100 meters). With the boat moored to the fixed buoy, the reef almost surfaces on your right when you face the bow of the vessel. South-west from this point is a series of coral pinnacles that almost reach the surface from a sandy sea bed at about 65 feet (20 meters). This area is good for those who do not intend to make a demanding dive. Enter the water from the boat and swim directly toward the nearby coral tops that are clearly visible in the transparent water. The most remarkable characteristic of this dive is the number of fissures and

cavities, often large enough for a diver, that cross the coral buttresses. Among these fissures, one in particular deserves a closer look. Large branches of gorgonians, one 10 feet (3 meters) wide, adorn its walls.

Proceed to the deepest dive along the external wall that plunges to great depths. The step where the sandy slope ends and the impressive continuous wall begins is just under the stern of the moored boat, depending on the wind. It is theoretically possible to descend directly to the sand and then follow the slope to the

F

E

G

H

C. Tabular acropora tend to choose the same type of sea bed, where large numbers settle in limited spaces.

D. This alcyonarian has outgrown the water's capacity to support it, and it therefore bends downward.

E. At some points the gorgonian sea fans grow so densely that they turn into impenetrable hedges.

F. As you get deeper, the hard formations become less rich, and gorgonian sea fans become dominant.

G. In spite of the effect caused by the wide-angle lens, these images reveal the extraordinary size reached by gorgonians in these waters.

H. A colony of soft corals projects into open water, challenging gravity.

edge, which is at a depth of more than 100 feet (30 meters).

It would be a serious error to turn right at this point and follow the wall northeast. In this direction the sloping sand surface is much more extended, and the dive would exceed no-decompression limits. Turn southwest, instead, and keep the wall to the left; even better, descend farther, beginning the dive from the coral pinnacles facing the impressive wall. This will let you make a comfortable ascent along an almost single wall from around 130 feet (40 meters).

PHOTOGRAPHY

This is another spectacular site for photography. Clear water and enormous gorgonians and alcyonarians on top of the coral pinnacle make it

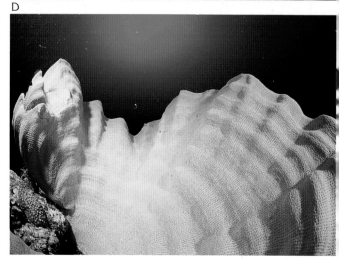

A. In the blue of deep waters, some reef walls seem to shine with their own light, actually the presence of numerous colonies of golden alcyonarians.

B. The acropora umbrellas sometimes seem to multiply, creating small umbrellas that rise in the center of the main colony.

C. The sponges rival hard corals, alcyonarians, and gorgonian sea fans in form and color.

D. This large laminate sponge resembles a colony of leaf-shaped hard coral.

easy. Use a wide-angle lens to capture the wonderful subjects along the wall and the rock arch on the plateau. To photograph the arch correctly, stand at the entrance that looks to the open sea, keeping it to your back, thus recovering some natural light and obtaining a subtle blue color in the opening. Don't forget to set a fairly slow exposure time.

E. The wide-angle lens clearly reveals the size of this gorgonian sea fan, which seems to reach all the way to the surface.

F. Large, golden alcyonarians are one of the most distinctive features of dives in the Coral Sea.

G. An alcyonarian with partially withdrawn polyps reveals the structure of its arborescent skeleton.

H. A diver is carefully exploring one of the numerous crevices in the sea beds of Rock Arch.

I. This sponge opens like a cup on the wall where it settled when it was a small larva. Favored by fate and by the good conditions, it has been able to grow to this size.

Scuba Zoo, Flinders Reef

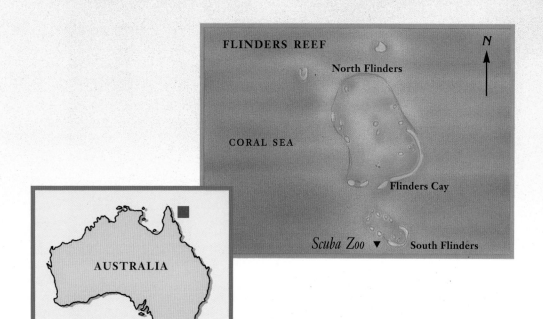

FLINDERS REEF

North Flinders

CORAL SEA

Flinders Cay

Scuba Zoo ▼   South Flinders

N

AUSTRALIA

INDIAN
OCEAN

0 ft
0 m

50 ft
15 m

Scuba Zoo is in the southern sector of South Flinders reef—more precisely, the part of South Flinders known by divers as South Boomer-ang Reef. The dive site is inside the lagoon on a sandy sea bed protected by the reef from the waves of the open ocean. Mike Ball Dive Expeditions has anchored an enormous antishark cage to the sea bed at 50 feet (15 meters).

A long, detailed briefing precedes this dive. The word *shark* always elicits a sense of anxiety and suspense. The idea of being in the middle of dozens of these magnificent creatures inspires feelings of fear and fascination in divers. The possible risk in this dive is minimal for sensible divers. The long briefing enhances the experience. It also addresses the worry of every boat crew that they will have to deal with someone rowdy, who creates dangers for himself and others. Don't

B

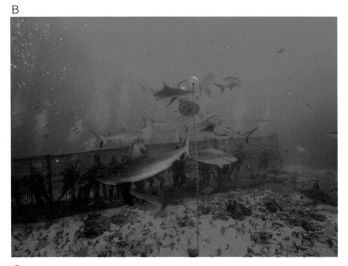

C

A. The barrel, which lets out a continuous stream of blood, is an irresistible attraction for the reef sharks, which have by now come to associate divers with offers of food.

B. Until the container is opened, the sharks merely swim around it in closer and closer circles.

C. A group of reef sharks circles the barrel, attracted by the bait it contains.

D. Protected by the cage, you can observe and photograph the sharks that swim faster and faster and become increasingly frenzied around the bait container.

A

D

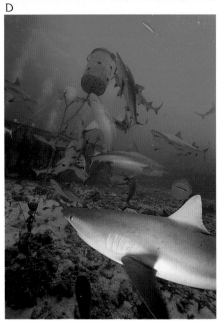

let yourself be intimidated, but follow the instructions carefully.

You will be told that two large cages are on the sea floor, set perpendicular to one another: one is 80 feet (25 meters) long, the other shorter. A smaller cage, with space for one or two divers, is placed in front of the longer one, more or less in the center. Between the tiny cage and the big one, a perforated bucket full of fish can be pulled by means of a system of pulleys, in order to introduce blood and odors into the water.

The divers are asked to get ready at the same time, jump into the water, and enter the cage rapidly from the large rear opening. The sharks associate the presence of the moored boat with food; some of them will be waiting for you. Each diver chooses a place inside the cage and, having taken care to weight himself properly, tries to stand as motionless as possible to prevent stirring up the water. When everyone is in place and the cages are closed, the bucket is thrown into the water and shaken with a rope from inside the large cage. This inevitably attracts the sharks, who begin their frenetic merry-go-round around the bait. This is the best time to observe them. The bucket is still closed and the sharks therefore merely circle elegantly for the moment. If the divers in the cage have been careful, visibility is quite good.

E. The sharks swim rapidly, grazing the sea bed in search of the last bait. The sharksuckers are now about to return to their customary places on the sharks.

After several minutes the dive-master in the cage pulls a rope and opens the bucket, which the sharks attack violently. A few minutes later everything is quiet once more. The sharks disappear as suddenly as they appeared, and the particles suspended in the water, agitated by the sharks' movements, begin to settle. The cages are opened and the divers can return to the boat unharmed.

PHOTOGRAPHY

Avoid very wide angles. They only serve to photograph the entire scene, including the cages. Lenses from 20 to 35 mm are excellent. Be careful not to get carried away and take one picture after another, consuming the entire roll of film in a few moments. Try to preadjust the camera for focus and exposure, and only take the picture when the animal is at the right distance and you have composed the frame properly.

Pay attention to the suspended particles. At the end of the dive, when the water is loaded with them, it may be worthwhile switching off the flash and working with environmental light, cutting exposure times to 1/125 of a second.

F. Whitetip reef sharks are one of the most common participants of shark feedings. It is always a surprise to see them so active; they are more commonly seen quietly at rest on the sea bed.

G. The odorous trace left by the bait can attract other large predators, such as barracuda, which prefer to linger nearby, aware that during the frenzy of the attack a stroke of a shark jaw could be fatal.

H. When the container is opened, the frenzy of the sharks reaches its peak. The sharksuckers also participate in the merry-go-round, abandoning their hosts to chase a shred of food.

China Wall, Flinders Reef

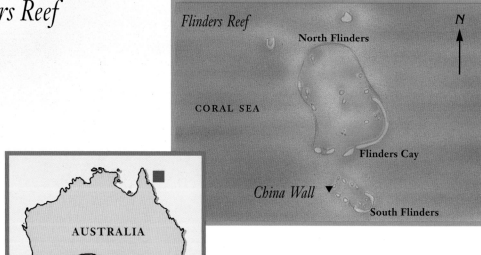

Flinders Reef
North Flinders
CORAL SEA
Flinders Cay
China Wall ▼
South Flinders
N

AUSTRALIA
INDIAN OCEAN

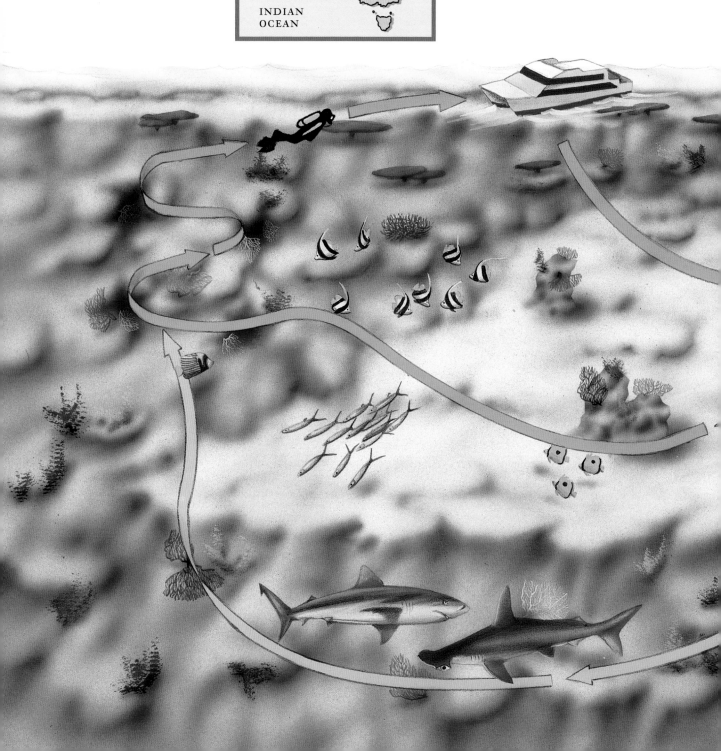

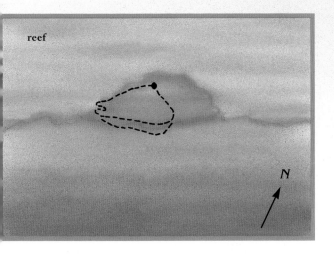

reef

N

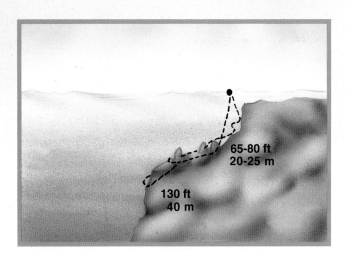

65-80 ft
20-25 m

130 ft
40 m

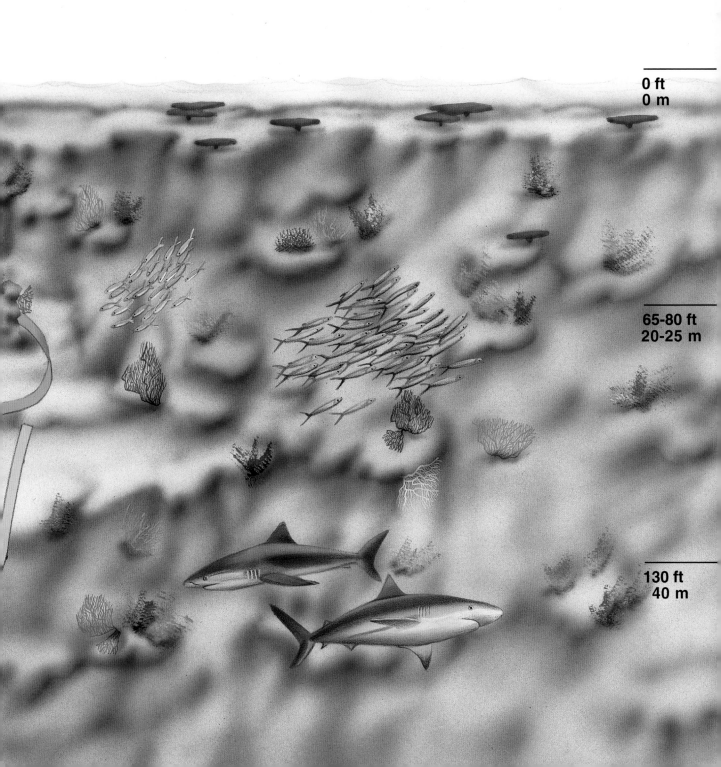

0 ft
0 m

65-80 ft
20-25 m

130 ft
40 m

China Wall is at the western tip of the arched barrier called North Boomer-ang Reef, south of the main reef at Flinders. This dive site is one of a series of fabulous dives along the endless walls typical of the Coral Sea.

A fixed mooring point indicates the dive site. From the surface you can see the mooring rope end in a large chain passed around a coral bommie. The boat moors over a sandy platform that slopes steeply and then drops vertically to an abyss of more than 3,280 feet (1,000 meters). A wide bay in the coral barrier has allowed the formation of a sandy slope at 15 to 33 feet (5 to 10 meters), which descends rapidly to greater depths southward. East and west of the mooring point, the great wall starts directly from the superficial buttresses of the coral barrier.

We recommend entering the water from the stern of the boat and descending directly toward the sandy sea bed at about 65 to 100 feet (20 to 30 meters). A descent at the bow along the mooring rope brings you to much greater depths. Once you have reached the sea floor, you can choose between two equally interesting routes, which actually justify two dives. In the first, you descend to great depths, swimming eastward along the wall to your left; in the second, you swim along the wall to your right to less demanding depths. If you plan to make two dives in these waters, you will do them in this sequence. You descend to about 130 feet (40 meters) on the first dive;

A

B

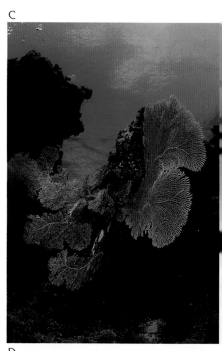

C

D

A. This large gorgonian sea fan hides the diver, but not his torch light.

B. Gorgonian sea fan forms can sometimes be oddly suggestive. This one, for instance, looks like a peacock tail.

C. The gorgonian sea fans that grow in large numbers along the endless walls of the Coral Sea seem to create a barrier hindering divers from going too deep.

D. The reef sometimes creates buttresses, in whose shade live large, softly colored alcyonarians.

magnificent branches of enormous gorgonians and brightly colored alcyonarians hang on the coral buttresses along with countless soft pink sponges. Rise gradually along the wall until you reach the reef's top. Return to the boat from here, taking time for a safety stop. On the second dive, you descend no more than 80 feet (25 meters) and concentrate on exploring the beautiful reef grottos between 80 and 50 feet (25 and 15 meters). Colored gorgonians grace these grottos, whose winding paths sometimes bring you near the surface.

PHOTOGRAPHY

Enormous walls, clear water, abundant alcyonarians and gorgonians, and the possibility of seeing large fish are all elements that call for wide-angle photography. In addition to classic images of gorgonians and walls, you should attempt to photograph inside the grottos. Try it without a flash, playing with the rays of light that penetrate through the cuts in the rock. To get good images of this kind you must carefully evaluate the available natural light. Take care not to be deceived by large areas of black in your frame. Concentrate on the penetrating blade of light. Approach the lighted area until it is the main feature in the frame, measure it, and use it as your reason to shoot, regardless of your position and frame.

E

F

G

H

E. The apparent monotony of this sandy sea bed is broken by coral blocks with large gorgonian sea fans.

F. A crinoid extends the net of its many branches, forming an intricate trap for organisms moving with the current.

G. Jacks always move in schools, following currents and beating the reef in search of prey.

H. Sharks swim by in the waters in front of the reef. They come from very great depths to venture close to the coral wall in search of easy prey.

Cod Wall, Flinders Reef

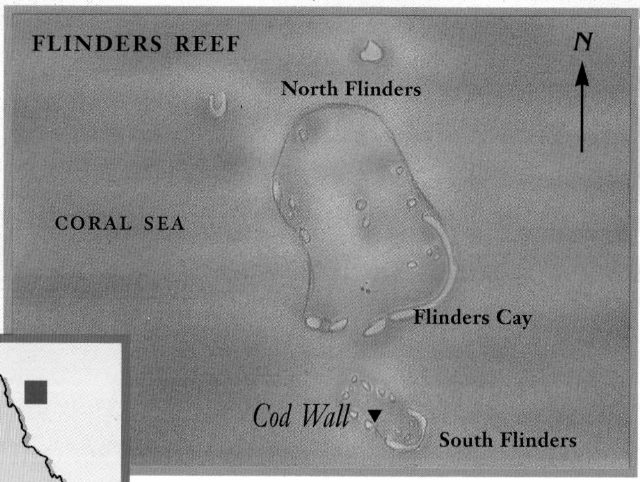

FLINDERS REEF

North Flinders

CORAL SEA

Flinders Cay

Cod Wall ▼   South Flinders

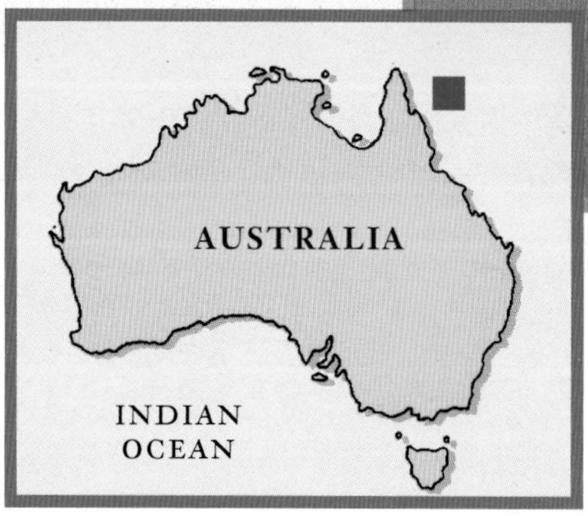

N

AUSTRALIA

INDIAN
OCEAN

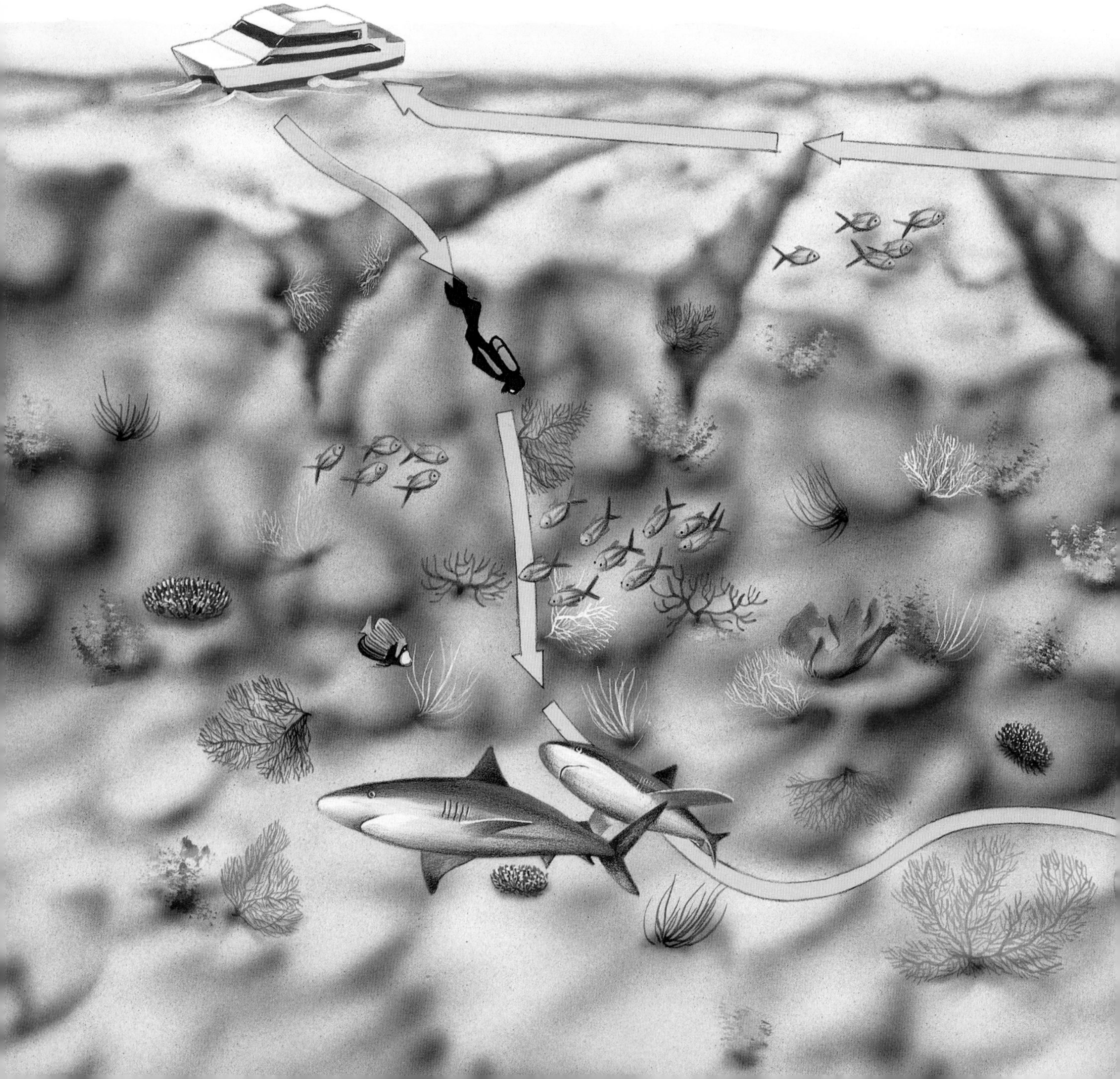

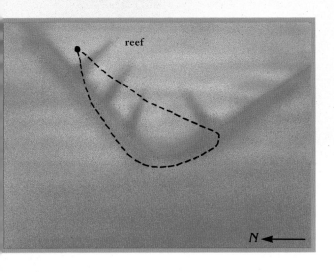

reef

N

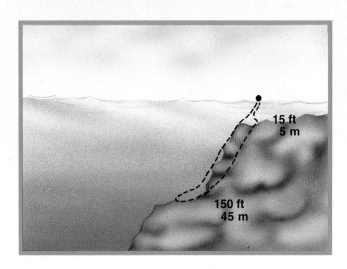

15 ft
5 m

150 ft
45 m

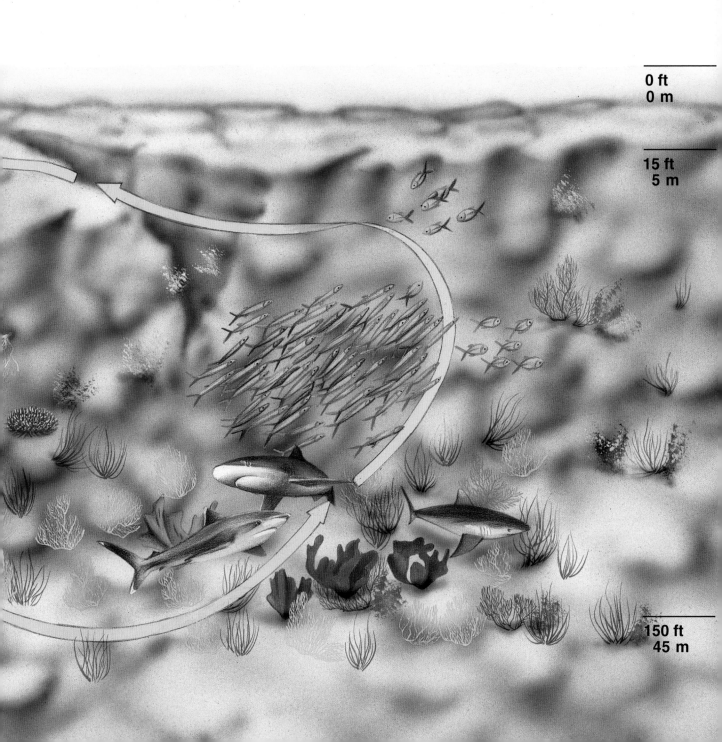

0 ft
0 m

15 ft
5 m

150 ft
45 m

A

B

C

This splendid dive takes place on an elliptical reef in South Flinders, also called South Boomerang. The fixed mooring point is in the southwestern section of the barrier, facing very deep sea beds. Owing to the orientation of the main reefs, Cod Wall is completely exposed to the southeastern winds; do not dive here when the wind is above 15 knots.

The dive at Cod Wall has many of the most typical Coral Sea features, only larger and more numerous. Incredible gorgonians 15 feet (5 meters) wide grow on this sea bed. There is an almost constant strong current here, so be prepared. The crew situates the boat to reduce the effects of the current, which can be intense. The prow of the boat is several feet from the coral barrier, which goes from 23 to 50 feet (7 to 15 meters); a sturdy line is fixed here. The current usually sweeps the wall, pushing your starboard side. Don't be intimidated by what you see on the surface. You enter the water from the stern and see, through very clear water, that the wall forms a pronounced angle at the end of the mooring line. Below you, there is a sandy plateau at 130 feet (40 meters), and in front of you, around the corner, the wall drops perpendicularly into the abyss of the Coral Sea. You descend rapidly, sheltered from the current by the great vertical wall, and aim for the sandy slope. Here, just below the edge, you will have no difficulty finding the gorgonian so enormous that it stands out clearly from the others. This is not to say that it is an isolated branch or that the surrounding fans are small! Swimming in this dense forest of gorgonians, among golden yellow fan shapes and intense red branches, is a magical experience. Elephant-ear sponges are very large and numerous here, too.

A. Sea whips, corals, and gorgonian sea fans grow inside a grotto with two openings, where there is a constant current.

B. This sand and gravel plain is studded with gorgonians and alcyonarians that oscillate under the currents.

C. This stretch of sea bed resembles a forest because of the dense growth of large gorgonian sea fans.

E

D

F

G

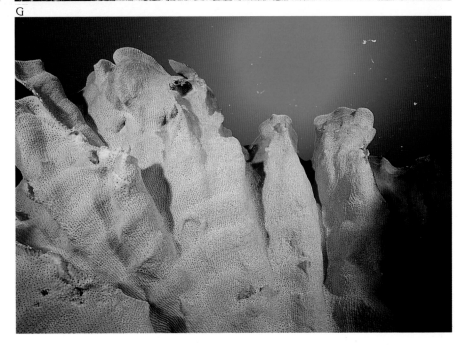

D. The limpid waters at Cod Wall reveal how the entire wall develops from sea bed to surface.

E. This level sea bed at about 130 feet (40 meters) is swept by a continuous current that favors luxuriant growth of many gorgonian varieties.

F. Elephant-ear sponges are quite abundant on this splendid reef, which features many distinctive elements of the Coral Sea.

G. These elephant-ear sponges form a compact, sinuous curtain whose contours resemble those of gorgonian sea fans and laminate coral blocks.

A

B

C

Continue swimming in the same direction, keeping the slope to your left, facing the current that sweeps through the gorgonian forest. It is surprisingly easy to find shelter on the sea bed and not be bothered at all by the current. Very soon you reach the middle of this marvelous wall, feeling tiny against the incred-ible forest of gorgonians. You are likely to see clouds of barracuda at around 100 feet (30 meters), speckling the deep blue sky above. At this depth there are many beautiful specimens of gray reef sharks. Even deeper, you

D

A. The force of the currents is one factor determining the distribution of the various species of gorgonians.

B. At this depth, which approaches the maximum permitted during sports dives, gorgonian sea fans colonize the entire sea bed.

C. The luxuriant gorgonians covering this tunnel have found an ideal habitat at depths less than 65 feet (20 meters).

D. Gorgonians and sponges create an impenetrable curtain along the sides of the sandy channels that cut through the coral.

may see the dark outlines of elusive hammerhead sharks.

While watching your time, depth, and air consumption, begin to ascend, once more swimming through the gorgonian forest. It is worthwhile to linger here, maybe watching a school of barracuda, before you head for the edge and return to the boat. Swim with the current, with the wall to your right. Here you swim above a series of deep channels, embellished with small arches and grottos full of fish, alcyonarians, and gorgonians. Rise slowly to the mooring rope at about 23 feet (7 meters).

PHOTOGRAPHY

It's hard to choose which photographic equipment to bring on the Cod Wall dive. Should you focus on photographing sponges and gorgonians, or sharks and barracuda? Every time we have dived at Cod Wall, we left our boat, the *Spoilsport*, on the site for the whole day; this way we have always been able to make two or more dives. You could concentrate on the gorgonians during the first dive, using a very wide-angle lens and two lamps, and on the fish during the second dive at less great depths.

E. This large gorgonian sea fan is bent by the current that runs close to the sea bed.

F. When photographing the gorgonians in these sea beds, use a wide-angle lens and at least two strobes.

G. Schools of silvery barracuda, with their tapering arrowlike form, swim in the deep blue waters surrounding the reef.

Dart Reef, Flinders Reef

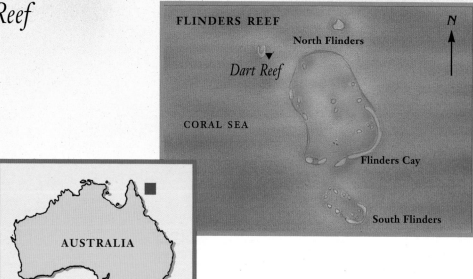

FLINDERS REEF
North Flinders
Dart Reef
CORAL SEA
Flinders Cay
South Flinders
N

AUSTRALIA

INDIAN
OCEAN

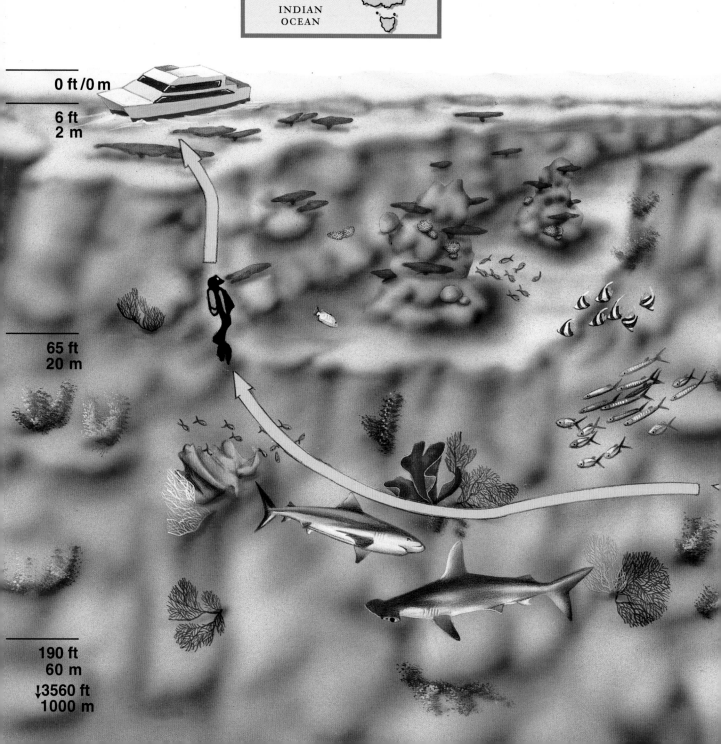

0 ft / 0 m

6 ft
2 m

65 ft
20 m

190 ft
60 m

↓3560 ft
1000 m

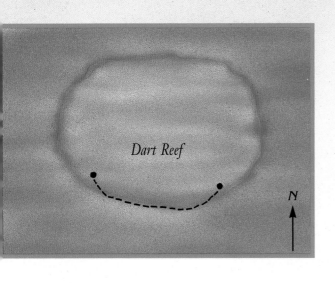

Dart Reef

N

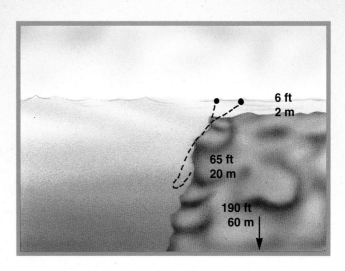

6 ft
2 m

65 ft
20 m

190 ft
60 m

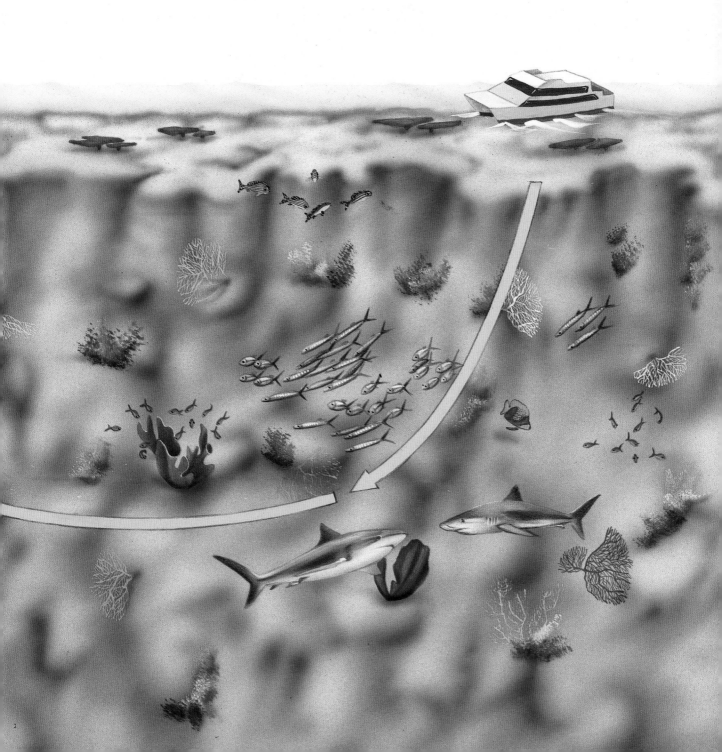

C

D art Reef is an impressive coral tower that rises from deeper than 2,950 feet (900 meters) to the surface, northeast of the much larger Flinders Reef. The coral shallow is solitary, large, compact, and massive. There is no lagoon with a shallow sea bed—it is surrounded by completely vertical walls. Prepare yourself for drift diving, because mooring is clearly impossible here. Considering the size of the reef— 4 miles (6 kilometers) in diameter— it is unthinkable to complete the entire circle underwater. The feasibility of every drift dive depends on the weather and the sea's condition. When there is a strong wind and high waves, it is impossible for the boat to approach the reef to let the divers enter the water; you don't want to risk losing a diver who may surface far from the barrier. Your patient wait for the right conditions will be amply rewarded by the fascinating scenario awaiting you underwater.

As soon as you have recovered from the impact with the water, you will be astonished by the immensity of the wall. It looks enormous and infinite in the transparent water. It feels like looking over a high mountain ledge. Your hands instinctively clutch whatever you are carrying for fear it will fall to unreachable depths. Begin swimming, keeping the wall to your right, and continue for a long stretch along the impressive wall. You have to descend quite deep to find the large isolated branches of gorgonians and alcyonarians. You will probably see some large oceanic specimens here, too. However, your attention will be drawn to the immensity of the wall and the sense of infinity you get when looking at the abyss below.

Pay especially close attention to your time, depth, and air consumption and begin to ascend. By now

A

D

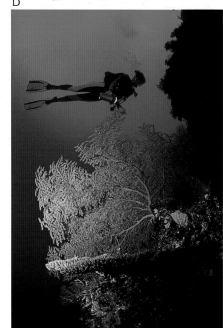

B

A. Despite their huge size, the gorgonian sea fans seem tiny in comparison with this wall, which extends for hundreds of feet.

B. Large branches of red gorgonians brighten the reef wall.

C. Soft corals and gorgonians draw your attention from the dark abyss beyond the almost vertical walls.

D. This image reveals the wall's structure — everything depends on coral building blocks. When corals die, they turn into hard rock on which other organisms can settle and grow.

E. This image focuses on a large gorgonian sea fan, but you can imagine the immensity of the surrounding environment.

F. Gorgonians inhabit this coral block, exemplifying the reef's coral composition.

G. The top of the impressive Dart Reef coral tower is colonized by large tabulate acropora that form wide umbrellas, dominating the other corals.

H. The waters surrounding the reef, where large schools of barracuda linger or swim, are as rich in life as the reef itself.

I. Jacks are typical oceanic fish often observed swimming in front of deep reefs.

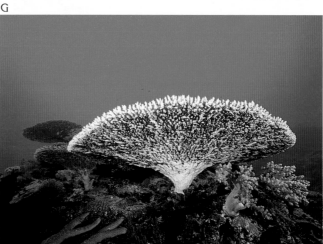

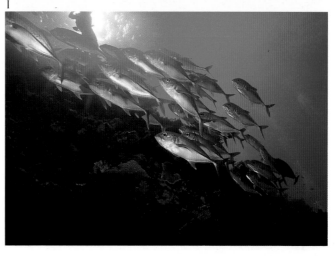

you should have reached a stretch of wall where wide channels of sandy sea bed incise the top plateau in the reef's center. The strong sensations that mark this dive slowly dissipate as you begin to swim in a more relaxing environment. The sand on the sea bed reflects the sunlight, and wonderful coral towers project upward from the center of the large channels. To finish the dive, all you need to do is rise along the lateral walls, rich in hard coral and coral blocks, and make a short safety stop on top of the plateau before you surface and swim to the boat.

PHOTOGRAPHY

Although it is difficult on dives like Dart Reef, try not to let yourself be carried away by the excitement. You will probably want to photograph everything you see in an attempt to render the immensity of the environment. The only way to give an idea of the proportions of the wall is to choose a well-defined subject in the foreground and leave the wall and a glimpse of blue in the background. A carefully chosen frame will help you to give some idea of the sensations experienced during this dive.

Myrmidon Reef

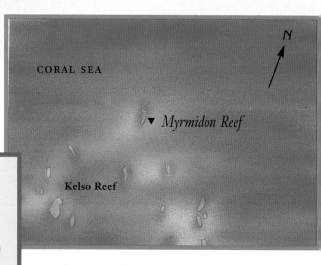

CORAL SEA

N

▼ *Myrmidon Reef*

Kelso Reef

AUSTRALIA

INDIAN
OCEAN

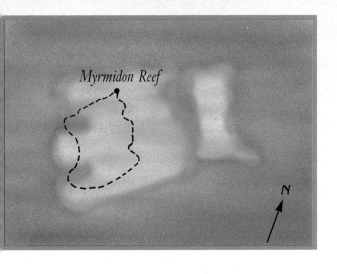

Myrmidon Reef

N

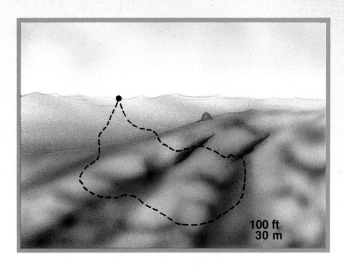

100 ft
30 m

0 ft
0 m

100 ft
30 m

This is quite a large reef just north of Townsville, the departure base for cruises to Flinders Reef. Many isolated coral groups form this area of the Great Barrier Reef. Myrmidon Reef sits on the border of the continental platform, facing sea beds that reach considerable depths. Diving is only possible here when the weather is good; the reef is totally exposed to the southeastern wind.

Myrmidon Reef boasts two of the most important and attractive traits of the dives off Coral Sea

B

C

A

D

E

A. This giant clam can just about resist the assault of the surrounding corals that bar its valves from every side.

B. Canyons and hills succeed one another in a varied environment ideal for diving and exploring reef life.

C. A deer-horn shaped acropora dominates one of the highest parts of the reef. Its structure allows it to resist the waves, often very strong in areas exposed to southeastern winds.

D. Particularly resistant acropora dominate the ridge of this stretch of coral sea bed. Less robust, larger forms grow on the walls.

E. A pair of small anemonefish or clownfish (Amphiprion melanopus) indicate that a sea anemone hides among the corals.

reefs: incredibly clear water and an extraordinary richness in hard corals. The spectacular view is right before your eye as soon as you enter the water. The sea bed below is more than 100 feet (30 meters) away, yet clearly visible down to the tiniest detail. In the distance, small waves break against the top of the coral barrier. From there, the coral blocks descend to great depths in a soft slope. This is a slow but constant grade, interrupted by valleys and ridges, sometimes incised by deep fissures that form canyons with borders engraved in coral. Compact, massive coral blocks, with the stockiest branches in small bushes, grow near the surface. The violent waves would destroy a more delicate structure—a slender carbonate lace would not survive a storm here. The waves are less violent at greater depths, and the tide arrives attenuated. The coral blocks can grow in height, assuming complex, ramified structures—very delicate forms protected by the mass of water above. Thanks to the clarity of the water, which lets the sunlight penetrate quite deeply, and to the softly sloping sea bed, which guarantees an abundance of space, conditions are ideal for incredible hard coral development. Myrmidon Reef probably has the most beautiful reef corals. There is no particular route to follow or any specific point to explore. You will definitely enjoy this dive and want to repeat it immediately. Just enter the water, swim to the sea bed under the boat at about 100 feet (30 meters), and begin to ascend the slope slowly, exploring the spectacular passages among the corals and admiring the sun's rays playing through the chiseled surfaces of the acropora. It is a long, enjoyable, and easy dive. Just north of Myrmidon Reef you can see the wreck of the *Foam*, which sank on February 5, 1893.

PHOTOGRAPHY

At Myrmidon Reef you will probably want to capture the vastness of the hard coral plain. Pay careful attention to the lighting: on a good day with bright sun and clear water, the vivid colors of the coral call for quite a closed aperture. Avoid photographing scenes with a wide-angle lens without including a subject in the foreground, such as your diving mate or a peculiar coral, which gives the image depth and proportion.

F

G

H

I.

F. The reef nearest the surface resembles an immense coral garden of countless species of hard coral.

G. A coral pinnacle is an ideal substratum for these laminate acropora.

H. In these waters, silvery barracuda (Sphyraena genie) form walls that reflect the sunlight like countless mirrors.

I. The extremely varied sea bed offers manifold habitats that enrich the variety of reef life. A large brain coral grows at the base of this wall, covered by gorgonians and acropora corals.

The Wreck of the Yongala

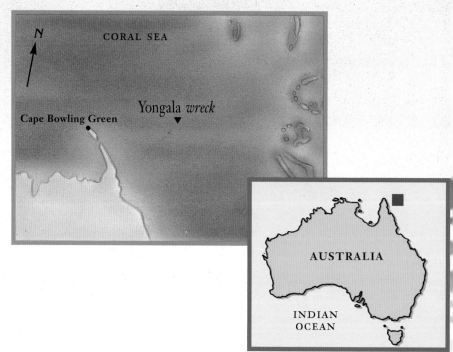

CORAL SEA

N

Cape Bowling Green

Yongala *wreck*

AUSTRALIA

INDIAN OCEAN

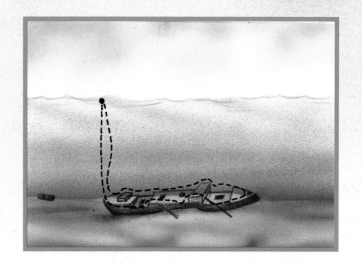

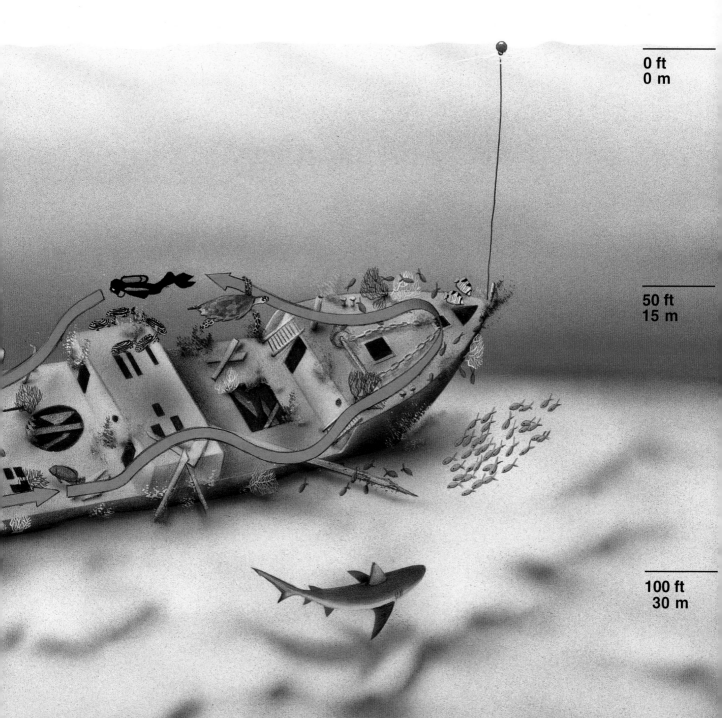

0 ft
0 m

50 ft
15 m

100 ft
30 m

The *Yongala* is located east of Townsville, off Cape Bowling Green. It lies inside the Great Barrier Reef's central area on a flat sandy sea bed at about 100 feet (30 meters). It is quite far from the coast and very complicated to find without exact geographic coordinates. We are not afraid of being contradicted when we say that the *Yongala* wreck is one of the most beautiful a diver will ever visit. What

D

A

E

B

F

C

A. Light filtering from the surface exposes the large wreck of the Yongala *in a fascinating way.*

B. In this image you see one of the extremities of the ship and its graceful line, which disappears into the blue water.

C. The outline of the hull reclined on the sea bed looks somewhat blurred through the particles in the water.

D. Turtles (Eretmochelys imbricata) are a constant presence at the Yongala. *The rich life evidently attracts these reptiles, who find a safe refuge in the wreck.*

E. One of the stingrays that inhabit the wreck, surprised while swimming above what it probably considers a good reef full of prey.

F. While sea snakes are not rare in this area, they do not represent a problem for divers unless provoked.

G. *A close-packed school of sweetlips swims in the wreck's shadow, looking for a spot to rest while waiting for nightfall.*

H. *A large eagle ray (Aetobatus narinari), distinguished by its maculate livery, swims over the Yongala wreck, flapping its fins.*

I. *A large school of young batfish swims in certain areas of the hull of the wreck.*

J. *Large numbers of jacks are attracted to this wreck. The underwater environment is particularly rich here because of the wreck's size and location on a flat sandy sea bed.*

makes this dive unique is that you can see an old, elegant, and well-preserved ship and at the same time feel the thrill of swimming among an incredible quantity of fish, some of them very large. There are also numerous snakes, turtles, and various marine mammals. A dive on the *Yongala* wreck means not only a trip into distant Australian seafaring history, but also a practical lesson on Coral Sea fish species.

Let us begin with the technical aspects of this sensational dive. The maximum depth is 100 feet (30 meters), where you meet the sandy sea floor. The ship's port side is at about 50 feet (15 meters) on the sand. The average depth on this dive is around 80 feet (25 meters). The environmental factors that affect this dive can pose some problems, however. Visibility is seldom exceptional and sometimes very poor in

I

J

G

H

these waters. Moreover, the area is almost constantly swept by currents, which are sometimes quite violent (probably the reason for the incredibly rich fauna). The crews of the charter boats are very careful when preparing for and executing a dive. Two buoys are fixed to the two extremities of the sunken ship to enable divers to descend and ascend safely in case of strong currents. This practice is less risky than trying to surface near the boat. When the current is unusually strong, the stern of the dive boat is often fixed to the buoy with a wire for the divers to use during ascent. The bridge structures on the wreck reduce the effects of the current.

The main technical aspects are described thoroughly during the dive briefing on the basis of current weather conditions. It is most important to be aware that the law of Queensland has for some years

A.

A. A grouper keeps a wary eye on a diver who approaches its territory.

B. In spite of many decades under water, the ship's structures are still well preserved, though transformed by the growth of marine organisms.

C. The bridge structures provide valuable shelter, reducing the effects of the sometimes quite violent currents.

D. Corroded by time and damaged by the violence of the wreck, the structure of the ship has large openings through which you can see the interior without venturing inside.

E. Numerous benthic organisms have settled on the solid hull beams, transforming the wreck into a small tropical reef.

B.

C.

D.

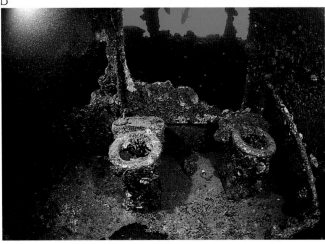

prohibited divers from entering the wreck, because the structures were gradually deteriorating from the actions of divers. So, don't forget to bring a torch or a strong light to illuminate the interior of the vessel, which is still loaded with goods. Once you have descended the buoy rope, begin to swim along the bridge, admiring the beautiful gorgonians and colored alcyonarians that colonize the metal. You will be amazed by the incredible quantity of fish of every size surrounding you in just a few feet of water. There are enormous trevallies, tropical sweetlips,

E.

dentexes, huge groupers, jacks, and a dense school of batfish. Tuna, enormous manta rays, eagle rays, sharks, and sometimes even whales and dolphins swim here. There are almost always large turtles and numerous sea snakes, too. Don't forget to have a look at the two extremities of the ship, which is more than 325 feet (100 meters) long, between the bow, the stern, and the hull. Incredibly big groupers and a dense school of sweetlips await you there, sheltered from the current.

PHOTOGRAPHY

The secret to taking pictures at the *Yongala* is to stay calm. Don't let yourself be carried away by the excitement, taking one photograph after another without proper care and attention, and rapidly exhausting your film. The water is loaded with

suspended particles and requires special attention when you set exposure time, aperture, and above all, the orientation of underwater flashes. Take care that the light of the flash comes from afar, arriving diffused and at the right angle, so it does not illuminate suspended particles violently, but merely gives a brush stroke of color to the subject without changing the natural light too much. Don't forget to take a few images of the ship's structure without a flash, taking care to aim the lens a bit upward when framing the image.

F. The orientation of this bridge enables divers to swim where passengers once walked.

G. A gorgonian and a large snapper: two typical inhabitants of the Yongala.

H. Evidence that the ship was once inhabited by humans can still be found here and there.

I. A large stingray, intrigued by the divers, emerges from the wreck's darkness.

J. The interior of the ship, now inaccessible, has become a fascinating labyrinth in which light and shade play.

THE FISH OF THE GREAT BARRIER REEF

It is not an easy task to present the diving of the Great Australian Barrier in a few lines. It is equally difficult to make a brief description of the thousands of fish species that live in these waters. The immense coral construction separating the Australian coastline and the Pacific Ocean was built by billions of tireless polyps extracting tons of calcium carbonate from the seawater over hundreds of millions of years. This structure is so vast that some say it is visible from the moon. It is not a single formation, but a galaxy of coral fragments that make up coral islands, which are inhabited by plants and birds, and atolls or band-shaped reefs, some of which surface, when the tide is low, from sea beds hundreds of feet below.

The Coral Sea embraces the outer Great Barrier Reef. To the south, the reefs spread out, lose uniformity, and gradually disappear in the cold Antarctic currents beyond the Bunker, Capricorn Island, and Lady Elliot Island. Still farther south, in the green waters of the Tasman Sea, Australian fur seals and small penguins swim among great kelp leaves —reminiscent of California's underwater scenes on the other side of the Pacific, more than 4,350 miles (7,000 kilometers) away. Only in this immense ocean could a stone garden like that of the Australian Great Barrier Reef grow. Everything here is gigantic, especially the invertebrates. Soft corals 7 feet (2 meters) tall are not rare; neither are gorgonian sea fans 15 feet (5 meters) wide, always surrounded by fish, coral blocks, starfish, and sea urchins. In just a few dozen square miles there are 900 species of fish, 100 types of coral and echinoderm, and hundreds of shellfish. Colored mantles of enormous giant clams (*Tridacna* sp.) resemble a blue wall against the bright coral blocks.

to adapt. However, we should all ensure that our interference does not become excessive. Considering the great size of these environments, it is hard to believe that people can leave palpable traces of their presence; yet many see this taking place. It is perhaps no coincidence that the interior of the *Yongala* wreck has been closed to divers to avoid further damage.

Diving along the variegated Australian reefs is like leafing through an enormous illustrated fish catalog. Choose any fish family: it is almost certainly represented by at least one species in these waters. The sharks here are particularly interesting: we begin with the white shark, perhaps the element most commonly associated with Australian waters, and then the various Carcharhinidae species found near the reefs and most often present during shark feedings—tiger sharks or leopard sharks with their long tails. Meeting a large manta ray with its long spined tail, or an eagle ray, or a giant manta ray can be a fascinating and unpredictable experience.

A widespread proliferation of tritons *(Charonia tritonis)*, merciless enemies of the spined starfish *(Acanthaster planci)*, was considered a threat to the coral barriers in the 1980s. The barrier preserved its equilibrium—a testament to our underestimation of its ability

While it is certainly no more risky to dive in these waters than elsewhere, and much more enjoyable, there are some dangers with which you would be wise to familiarize yourself. Most divers are

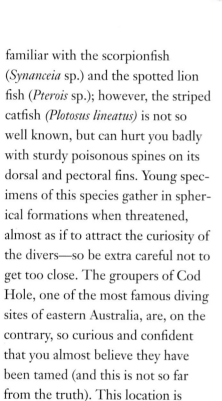

familiar with the scorpionfish (*Synanceia* sp.) and the spotted lion fish (*Pterois* sp.); however, the striped catfish *(Plotosus lineatus)* is not so well known, but can hurt you badly with sturdy poisonous spines on its dorsal and pectoral fins. Young specimens of this species gather in spherical formations when threatened, almost as if to attract the curiosity of the divers—so be extra careful not to get too close. The groupers of Cod Hole, one of the most famous diving sites of eastern Australia, are, on the contrary, so curious and confident that you almost believe they have been tamed (and this is not so far from the truth). This location is home to a family of giant groupers of the *Epinephelus tukula* species that can weigh up to 440 pounds (200 kilograms), but that move in the water with the agility of dancers. They come so close that they almost touch your face, waiting for some food, which they rapidly suck into their large mouths.

In other areas, in the midst of a kaleidoscope of forms and colors formed by alcyonarians, corals, gorgonians, ascidians, and sponges (such as the enormous elephant ears), the variety of fish is impressive. Many types of angelfish—*Chaetodon auriga*, *C. lunula, Heniochus acuminatus*—are common, as well as the tiny *Centropyge* angelfish (*C. bicolor* and *C. bispinosus*) and the horned batfish *(Platax batavianus)*, which owes its name to the frontal protuberance it develops as an adult. Among the snappers we cannot forget the hussar fish *(Lutjanus adetii)*, with its typical yellow band, almost a coat of arms; these fish gather in orderly ranks in shaded areas of the reef, where you also come across tropical sweetlips, damselfish, chromis, gobies, triggerfish, blennies, cardinalfish, boxfish, and pufferfish. And these are only a few in the long list of fish that live in this area.

Diving among the corals inevitably makes you look toward the sea bed, but there is life behind you, too. The waters near the barrier, which often look to abysses of hundreds of feet, must hide millions of old fossilized corals. They are populated by trevallies, barracuda, tuna, and cetaceans; although they can move rapidly, these species seem to have chosen certain areas of the barriers in particular, probably because of the abundance of prey. It is in this prodigious life, starting with the small polyps of the coral blocks, that the secret and charm of the barrier lies.

Whale shark
Rhincodon typus

Largest fish in the world; can exceed 40 feet (12 meters). Easily recognizable by its bluish color, large white spots, and body covered with longitudinal stripes; mouth in a frontal position. Feeds exclusively on plankton and small fish. Harmless, despite its size.

LAMNIDAE FAMILY

Great white shark
Carcharodon carcharias

Robust body quite wide at the front; short pointed snout; large mouth armed with clearly triangular teeth, especially in upper jaw. Grayish upper body; white belly. Feeds on fish or, when large, on cetaceans. Can measure over 23 feet (7 meters). Rarely seen in the region but considered dangerous to humans.

CARCHARHINIDAE FAMILY

Tiger shark
Galeocerdo cuvieri

Robust body; distinctive short, rounded snout; wide mouth armed with characteristic serrated, subtriangular teeth; caudal fin has large upper lobe that tends to narrow at the tip. Dorsal region grayish brown in color; white belly; lateral stripes typical in young individuals. Feeds on a great variety of prey, as well as on detritus. Grows to 17 feet (5.5 meters).

Bull shark
Carcharhinus leucas

Robust, compact body; short, rounded snout; wide mouth with upper jaw armed with triangular, jagged teeth; well-developed pectoral fins with indented back edge; second dorsal fin and anal fin alike and opposite. Gray dorsal region; whitish belly. Lives near the coast and will venture into shallow waters. Feeds on fish, rays, and small sharks. Considered dangerous to humans. Grows to 12 feet (3.5 meters).

Whitetip oceanic shark
Carcharhinus longimanus

Tapered, robust body; clearly rounded, white-tipped fins; particularly large and wide pectoral fins; short rounded snout. Lives near the surface and rarely ventures near the coast. Back is grayish in color; whitish belly. Feeds on fish and squid. Grows to 9 feet (2.7 meters).

▶

ORECTOLOBIDAE FAMILY

Carpet shark
Orectolobus ornatus

▼

Flattened body adapted to life on the sea bed; wide mouth surrounded by long irregular papillae; protractile jaws armed with large piercing teeth. Coloration features characteristic variegated spots and patches. Nocturnal and feeds on fish and invertebrates; lives on coralline sea beds from several feet down to about 100 feet (30 meters). Grows to 9 feet (2.7 meters).

MOBULIDAE FAMILY

Giant manta
Manta birostris

Wide body; ventrally flattened back. Easily distinguished by large cephalic fins at sides of mouth; quite well developed pectoral fins permit the fish to reach a width of 15 to 20 feet (5 to 6 meters). Often sighted at edge of reefs and above deep sea beds, where it follows plankton masses, on which it feeds.

▶

DASYATIDAE FAMILY

Bluespotted ribbontail stingray
Taeniura lymma

◀ Disc-shaped body, flattened and slightly elongated. Yellowish brown back with characteristic blue spots. Tail has one or two robust, poisonous spines. Typical in sandy areas among coralline formations. Often sighted under acropora umbrellas or at cave entrances. Feeds on crustaceans and mollusks. Grows up to 7 feet (2.4 meters) long, including the tail.

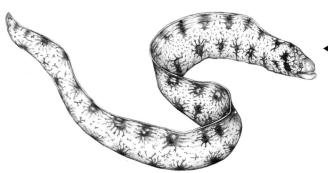

Marbled moray
Gymnothorax undulatus

Medium-sized moray with pointed snout, narrow jaws, and large eyes; front nostrils are quite evident. Generally recognized by yellowish color on upper part of head and marbled stripes on body. Prefers detrital beds of lagoons and crevices on reefs up to 65 to 100 feet (20 to 30 meters). Feeds on fish and octopuses, which it captures at night. Grows to 4 feet (1.5 meters) in length.

MURAENIDAE FAMILY

◄ Snowflake moray
Echidna nebulosa

Tapered, slender body; short snout with pointed jaws; conical front teeth are short and sturdy; lateral teeth resemble molars. Whitish in color, with two rows of black spots speckled with yellow, scattered with smaller black spots. Lives on low and flat rock or coral sea beds. Feeds principally on crustaceans. Active mainly at night and seems attracted to light. Measures up to 30 inches (75 centimeters).

►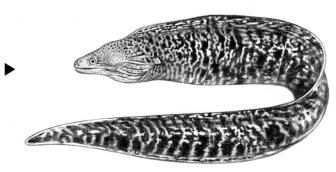

◄ Honeycomb moray
Gymnothorax favagineus

Large moray with characteristic black spots separated by white stripes that look like beehive cells. Lives along the outer slopes of reefs from 100 to 115 feet (30 to 35 meters). Feeds primarily on fish. Can exceed 6 feet (1.8 meters) in length.

PLOTOSIDAE FAMILY

Striped catfish
Plotosus lineatus

Elongated body; second dorsal fin extends to the tail, where it joins the anal fin, which is also quite developed; snout has four pairs of barbels; pointed poisonous spines in front of pectoral fins and first dorsal fin. Coloration features white, longitudinal stripes. Young individuals are gregarious; adults are solitary. Feeds on small invertebrates. Reaches a length of almost 13 inches (32 centimeters).

►

SYNODONTIDAE FAMILY

Lizardfish
Synodus variegatus

Tapered, cylindrical body; snout has profile that resembles the head of a lizard; narrow mouth with pointed teeth. Varies in color from brownish to red. Usually lives between 13 and 130 feet (4 and 40 meters) near coral blocks, where it lies in wait for the fish on which it feeds. Grows to 8 inches (20 centimeters).

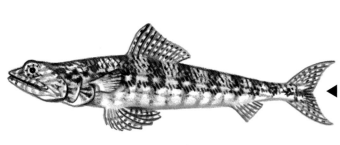

ANTENNARIIDAE FAMILY

Hispid frogfish
Antennarius hispidus

▶

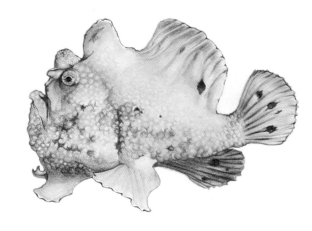

Rounded, globose body, tall and compressed in the rear; mouth turns upward; dorsal fin has long mobile ray, which serves as bait. Coloration varies from yellowish to orange brown. Feeds on small fish and shellfish. Lives close to rocks and corals up to 295 feet (90 meters). It grows to a length of 7 inches (18 centimeters).

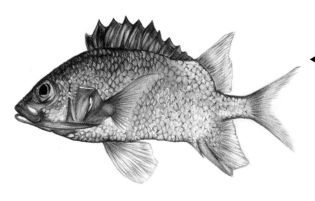

Doubletooth soldierfish
Myripristis hexagona

Oval, moderately compressed, tall body covered with large scales; extremity of the lower jaw characterized by grouped teeth; large eyes. Coloration is reddish; fin borders are whitish. Mostly active at night; lives among reef recesses to a depth of 80 feet (25 meters). Measures up to 8 inches (20 centimeters).

HOLOCENTRIDAE FAMILY

◀ ### Blotcheye soldierfish
Myripristis murdjan

Oval, moderately compressed, wide body, covered with large spiny scales; first dorsal fin has robust spiny rays; large eyes. Coloration is red; fin tips are darker than body. Nocturnal and lives among reef crevices up to 115 to 130 feet (35 to 40 meters). Grows to almost 11 inches (27 centimeters).

▶

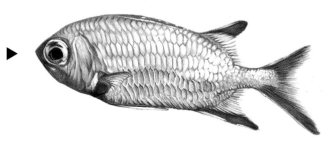

◀ ### White-tail squirrelfish
Sargocentron caudimaculatum

Oval, compressed body; pointed snout; long robust caudal peduncle; large eyes. Front portion is reddish; back is silvery white; white lower edge of dorsal fin. Nocturnal and lives among reef crevices between 20 and 130 feet (6 and 40 meters). Grows up to 10 inches (25 centimeters).

Red squirrelfish
Sargocentron rubrum

Oval, compressed body; pointed snout; long robust caudal peduncle; large eyes. Coloration marked by horizontal streaks alternately white-silvery and brownish; dorsal fin features central white stripe. Active at night; lives among reef recesses between 10 and 80 feet (3 and 25 meters). Grows to almost 11 inches (27 centimeters).

▶

ANOMALOPIDAE FAMILY

Small flashlight fish
Photoblepharon palpebratus

Sturdy, oval body terminates in a long peduncle that supports a clearly forked tail; characterized by luminous organs below the eyes, which can be turned off by special flaps of skin. Usually sighted on moonless nights along reef walls full of caves. Grows to almost 5 inches (12 centimeters).

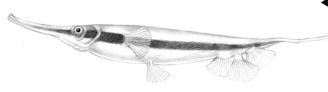

SYNGNATHIDAE FAMILY

Schultz's pipefish
Corythoichthys schultzi

Slender, elongated body; bony rings running lengthwise; elongated, terminal, tubular mouth; small fins. Whitish in color with dark spots and stripes; pink caudal fin. Lives among corals between 10 and 80 feet (3 and 25 meters). Grows up to 6 inches (15 centimeters).

CENTRISCIDAE FAMILY

◀ Razorfish
Aeoliscus strigatus

Extremely compressed body, pointed snout; slender tail. Can camouflage itself among sea urchins' spines or coral branches, thanks to special body form. Whitish or reddish in color with a longitudinal band on flanks. Lives near the sea floor between 3 and 50 feet (1 and 15 meters). Grows up to 6 inches (15 centimeters).

◀ Spotted seahorse
Hippocampus kuda

Unmistakable form: bony plates with small protuberances cover the body. Coloration varies according to surroundings. Lives along coastal reefs and in brackish waters to 100 feet (30 meters). Measures up to 12 inches (30 centimeters) .

SCORPAENIDAE FAMILY

Scorpionfish
Scorpaenidae synanceia

Sturdy body; raised dorsal region; wide upturned mouth. Coloration is mimetic, but brightly colored inner portion of pectoral fins is displayed as warning; dorsal fin's rays are poisonous. Lives on algae-covered or detrital sea beds to 230 feet (70 meters). Measures up to 12 inches (30 centimeters).

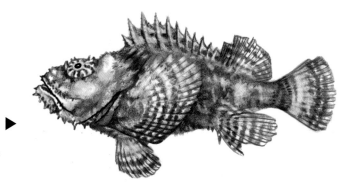

Stonefish
Synanceia verrucosa

Compact, robust body; concave head; almost vertical mouth. Color and body shape render extremely poisonous spines nearly invisible—a true danger of tropical seas. Measures up to 14 inches (36 centimeters).

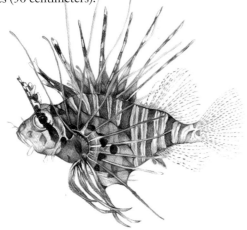

Spotted lionfish
Pterois antennata

Very typical of species: extremely developed rays on dorsal and pectoral fins and long tentacles above the eyes; poisonous spines on fins. Coloration features brownish red vertical stripes on the body. Feeds mainly on crustaceans. Prefers shaded areas up to 50 feet (15 meters). Measures 9 inches (24 centimeters).

SERRANIDAE FAMILY

Purple anthias
Pseudanthias tuka

Tapered body; clearly forked tail. Both sexes are purple in color. Males have a red spot at base of dorsal fin, a more developed upper lip, and are elongated to the back. Females have a yellow stripe on the back and yellow-edged caudal fins. Forms dense schools at edges of outer reef and in lagoon channels. Grows to 5 inches (12 centimeters).

Redmouth grouper
Aethaloperca rogaa

Wide, compressed; almost quadrangular body; back of head is concave. Dark brown or black in color with a lighter band along underside. Shy and tends to remain hidden in reef caves at 165 to 180 feet (50 to 55 meters). Grows to 24 inches (60 centimeters).

Coral grouper
Cephalopholis miniata

Tapered, robust body, slightly compressed at the sides. Common in the clearest waters and along channels that cross the reef. Feeds primarily on fish. Grows to 16 inches (40 centimeters).

Potato grouper
Epinephelus tukula

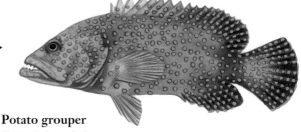

Robust, compact body; tapered head slightly indented between the eyes; wide mouth with overdeveloped lower jaw. Whitish in color with large, dark rectangular spots. Feeds primarily on fish. Lives on the coral sea floor between 15 and 490 feet (5 and 150 meters). Grows to 5.5 feet (2 meters).

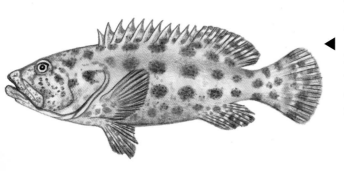

Spotted grouper
Epinephelus tauvina

Elongated body; robust, large head; wide mouth extends back beyond the eye. Greenish gray with red tones more evident on the fins. Feeds on fish. Lives on coralline sea beds between the surface and 165 feet (50 meters). Grows to 30 inches (75 centimeters) .

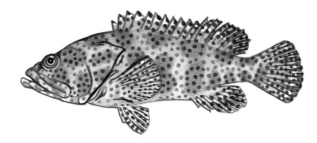

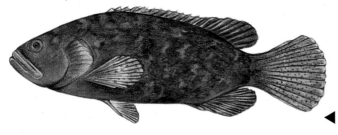

Giant grouper
Epinephelus lanceolatus

Massive, tapered body; very wide mouth; low dorsal fin with slightly pointed rear margin. Coloration is brownish in adults; young specimens have typical black and yellow spots. Lives in lagoons, along reefs, and in wrecks up to 325 feet (100 meters). Grows up to 9 feet (2.7 meters).

PLESIOPIDAE FAMILY

Comet
Calloplesiops altivelis

Elongated body; wide mouth; large eyes; dorsal and anal fins quite developed and almost seem joined to very wide, rounded caudal fin. Blackish in color with many small light spots. Characteristic large black spot edged in white at end of dorsal fin. When it takes refuge in a crevice, it leaves its tail out, and the spot looks like a large moray head. Grows to 6 inches (16 centimeters).

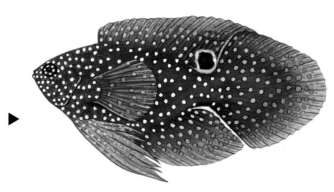

APOGONIDAE FAMILY

Seven-striped cardinalfish
Apogon novemfasciatus

Oval, compressed, elongated body; robust caudal peduncle; double dorsal fin; small mouth. Coloration features dark longitudinal streaks converging on tail. Lives chiefly in lagoons rich in coral up to 14 feet (4 meters). Measures up to 3.5 inches (9 centimeters).

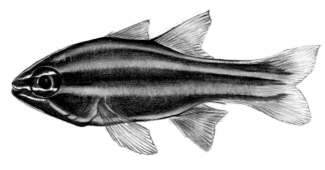

Pajama cardinalfish
Sphaeramia nematoptera

Oval, compressed, wide body; quite large dorsal fins. Yellow head with reddish eyes and a vertical black band between first dorsal and ventral fins; back of head is spotted. Lives among branching corals at 15 to 20 feet (5 to 6 meters). Grows to 3 inches (8 centimeters).

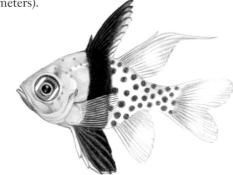

PRIACANTHIDAE FAMILY

Bloch's bigeye
Priacanthus blochii

Oval, tall, compressed body; short snout partly covered by large eyes; mouth turns upward; only one dorsal fin; rounded margin on caudal fin. Coloration is pink with irregular red spots. Chiefly nocturnal; lives in shaded areas between 50 and 100 feet (15 and 30 meters). Grows to 14 inches (35 centimeters).

ECHENEIDAE FAMILY

Sharksucker
Echeneis naucrates

Elongated body flattened on dorsal region. Typically associated with larger fish, such as sharks and manta rays, to which it adheres using sucker on dorsal fin. Feeds on parasites from host fish, but capable of swimming and hunting independently. Measures up to 3.5 feet (1.1 meters).

CARANGIDAE FAMILY

Indian threadfin
Alectis indicus

Very compressed body, tall in front, tapered in the rear; crescent-shaped tail; short snout with markedly blunt profile; caudal peduncle features small lateral keels; similar dorsal and anal fins are situated opposite one another. Silvery in color. Young specimens often associate with jellyfish; adults live at depths of nearly 200 feet (60 meters). Measures over 5 feet (1.7 meters).

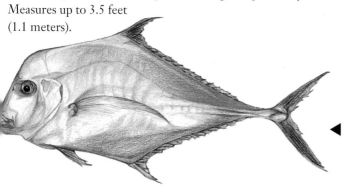

LUTJANIDAE FAMILY

Bluestriped snapper
Lutjanus kasmira

Tapered, compressed body; pointed snout; forked tail. Distinguished by longitudinal blue stripes along flanks. May form schools of up to 100 individuals, feeding around isolated coral pinnacles or shipwrecks. Nocturnal; takes shelter by day among corals. Measures up to 14 inches (35 centimeters).

Two-spot red snapper
Lutjanus bohar

Tapered, somewhat wide body; pointed snout rounded at the top; slightly indented caudal fin. Dorsal region is dark brown or blackish. Feeds on fish, crustaceans, and mollusks. Lives in open waters along reefs between 50 and 655 feet (15 and 200 meters). Measures up to 30 inches (75 centimeters).

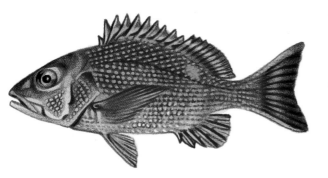

Humpback red snapper
Lutjanus gibbus

Compact, wide, compressed body; pointed snout; in larger individuals dorsal profile has characteristic hollow at eye level; preoperculum has a deep incision; clearly indented caudal fin has rounded lobes. Brownish green in color on the back, with reddish flanks and underside; yellow eyes, lips, and base of pectoral fins. Lives in schools in relatively deep water along the reef. Feeds on benthic invertebrates and fish. Reaches 24 inches (60 centimeters) in length.

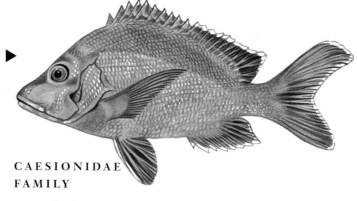

CAESIONIDAE FAMILY

Lunar fusilier
Caesio lunaris

Tapered body, slightly compressed at the sides; clearly forked tail; slightly protractile mouth. Bluish silver in color with a black-tipped tail. Lives in schools in waters near the outer slopes of reefs between 15 and 100 feet (5 and 30 meters). Measures up to 12 inches (30 centimeters).

HAEMULIDAE FAMILY

Harlequin sweetlips
Plectorhynchus chaetodonoides

Tall sturdy body, compressed laterally; head convex on dorsal side; subterminal mouth with large lips and small conical teeth. Young specimens (illustrated here) are brown with large white spots; adults are speckled with black. Usually lives at the base of corals or in grottos to a depth of 100 feet (30 meters). Feeds on benthic invertebrates. Measures up to 29 inches (72 centimeters).

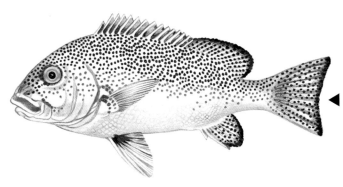

Spotted sweetlips
Plectorhynchus picus

Robust body, compressed at the sides; rounded convex head; subterminal mouth with large lips and small conical teeth; slightly indented tail. Young individuals are white with wide black bands that merge into each other; adults have dense dark spots. Solitary and lives at the base of coral formations or in caves to a depth of 165 feet (50 meters). Feeds on crustaceans. Measures up to 33 inches (84 centimeters).

LETHRINIDAE FAMILY

Striped emperor
Lethrinus nebulosus

Elongated, somewhat compressed body with pointed snout and slightly concave profile; wide, slightly indented caudal fin. Yellowish bronze in color with small blue spots on scales. Solitary or lives in small schools near the reef at depths of between 15 and 245 feet (5 and 75 meters). Grows to 32 inches (80 centimeters).

MULLIDAE FAMILY

Yellowstriped goatfish
Mulloidichthys flavolineatus

Elongated and compressed body; short snout of oblique profile. Barbels by the mouth of average length. Bright coloration, with longitudinal yellow stripe and a black spot on the flank, which sometimes disappears. Lives on sandy sea beds, sometimes in large groups, to a depth of 115 feet (35 meters). Grows to 17 inches (43 centimeters).

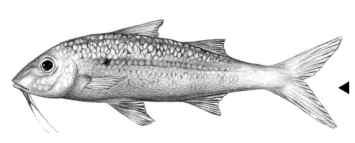

Spotted goatfish
Parupeneus barberinus

Elongated, compressed body; long snout with slightly concave profile. Mouth has well-developed barbels; clearly forked tail. Light in color, with dark longitudinal stripe along the flanks from mouth to caudal peduncle, which is decorated by one spot. Lives in small schools on sandy sea beds to a depth of 325 feet (100 meters). Grows to 24 inches (60 centimeters).

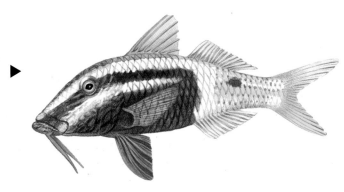

PEMPHERIDAE FAMILY

Pigmy sweeper
Parapriacanthus ransonneti

Oval, compressed body with large eyes and small, upturned mouth. Like the cardinal fish, it has only one dorsal fin. Whitish and translucent in color, with a yellowish head. Lives in schools in caves or poorly illuminated areas from 15 to 5 to 130 feet (40 meters). Grows to 4 inches (10 centimeters).

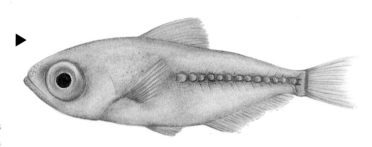

EPHIPPIDAE FAMILY

Batfish
Platax teira

Compressed, wide, almost disc-shaped body with well-developed dorsal and anal fins. Small terminal mouth has teeth like brushes, which it uses to scrape algae and small invertebrates from the sea floor. Primarily distinguished by one black spot in front of anal fin. Common in lagoons. Adults live in pairs. Grows to 24 inches (60 centimeters).

Red-faced batfish
Platax pinnatus

Compressed, wide, almost disc-shaped body with well-developed dorsal and anal fins. Snout has a hollow at eye level; small terminal mouth. Silvery in color, with two blackish bands on snout and in front portion of the body. Solitary and lives along the reef to a depth of 65 feet (20 meters). Grows to 18 inches (45 centimeters).

CHAETODONTIDAE FAMILY

Spot-nape butterflyfish
Chaetodon oxycephalus

Compressed, rounded body; somewhat convex, pointed snout; small terminal mouth. Whitish coloration with yellow band; black spot on the rear. Eyes masked by a black band that precedes a black spot on the nape. Lives in pairs along the reef at 33 to 130 feet (10 to 40 meters). Measures up to 10 inches (25 centimeters).

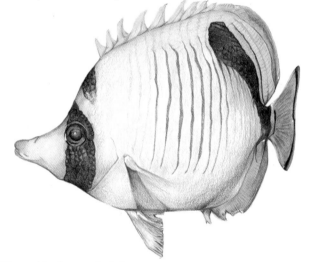

Threadfin butterflyfish
Chaetodon auriga

Subrectangular body, quite wide and compressed. Head is concave in front and ends in a short, pointed snout. A broad dark band covers the eye and narrows along the back. Dark ocellar spot along back edge of dorsal fin, surmounted by several elongated, thready rays typical of this species. Solitary or lives in pairs. Grows to 10 inches (25 centimeters).

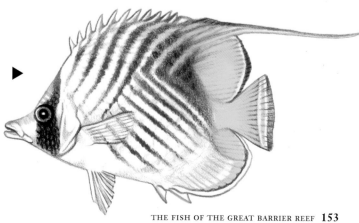

Raccoon butterflyfish
Chaetodon lunula

Compressed, rounded body with oblique, pointed snout; small terminal mouth. Yellow with a black band on the eyes and an oblique band at the back of the head; caudal peduncle has a black spot. Lives along the reef to depths of 100 feet (30 meters). Grows to 8 inches (20 centimeters).

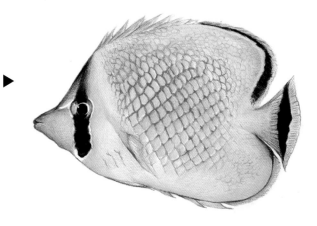

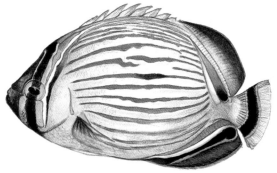

Redfin butterflyfish
Chaetodon trifasciatus

Compressed, oval body; pointed snout; small terminal mouth. Yellowish white coloration with thin purple streaks on flanks; eyes covered by a black band. Territorial and lives in pairs in protected areas rich in coral to a depth of 65 feet (20 meters). Measures up to 6 inches (15 centimeters).

Latticed butterflyfish
Chaetodon rafflessi

Compressed, oval body of average height; pointed snout; small terminal mouth. Yellow coloration with a thin, dark, gridlike pattern on flanks; eyes masked by a black band that continues to the nape; black spot on tail. Lives in pairs in areas rich in coral to a depth of 50 feet (15 meters). Grows to 6 inches (15 centimeters).

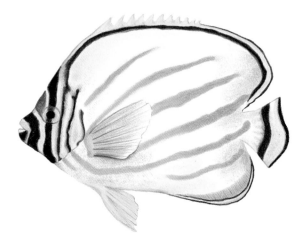

Ornate butterflyfish
Chaetodon ornatissimus

Compressed, somewhat wide and oval body; small terminal mouth. Light colored with oblique orange stripes; head decorated with black stripes that mask the eyes. Adults are territorial and live in pairs, alternating between coral-rich areas and open water to depths of 130 feet (40 meters). Grows to 8 inches (20 centimeters).

Copper-banded butterflyfish
Chelmon rostratus

Compressed, wide body, truncated at the back; elongated snout with narrow jaws. Its basic color is whitish, with narrow, vertical orange bands; black spot at base of dorsal fin. Often lives in pairs on coralline sea beds and in sandy areas to depths of 80 feet (25 meters). Grows to 8 inches (20 centimeters).

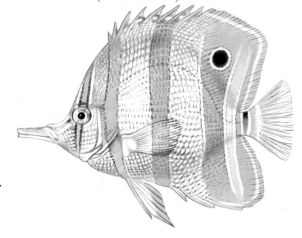

Long-nosed butterflyfish
Forcipiger flavissimus

Compressed body that ends with a long snout; dorsal fin has well-developed, separate rays; ventral fins thready and extend beyond the base of the anal fin. Almost entirely yellow in color, with black spot at base of tail; upper part of snout is black, lower part whitish in color. Feeds on protruding appendages of benthic invertebrates with its long snout. Grows up to 9 inches (22 centimeters).

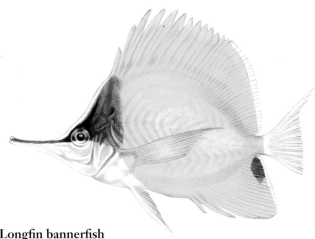

POMACANTHIDAE FAMILY

Emperor angelfish
Pomacanthus imperator

Wide, elongated body; slightly flattened snout; mouth has overdeveloped lower jaw. Diagonal yellow and bluish stripes on flanks; yellow caudal fin. Young individuals have light and blue concentric bands. Feeds on sponges and algae. Territorial and tends to be solitary, living between 10 and 230 feet (3 and 70 meters). Grows up to 16 inches (40 centimeters).

Longfin bannerfish
Heniochus acuminatus

Wide, compressed body; pointed snout concave at the back; clearly raised back ends in a dorsal fin with long sickle-shaped rays that fold back beyond the small caudal fin. Adults generally live in pairs in deep areas of reef and lagoon. Young individuals also act as cleaner fish. Grows up to 10 inches (25 centimeters).

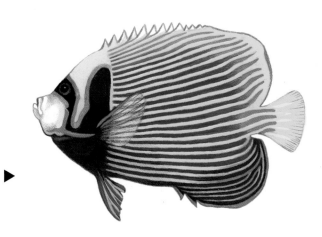

Koran angelfish
Pomacanthus semicirculatus

Wide, elongated body; slightly flattened snout; thick lips; pointed back edge on dorsal fin. Bluish in color; light blue stripes on opercula; fins edged with yellow. Young individuals have alternating white and blue bands. Feeds on sponges and algae. Territorial and solitary; lives at depths of 10 to 100 feet (3 to 30 meters). Grows up to 15 inches (38 centimeters).

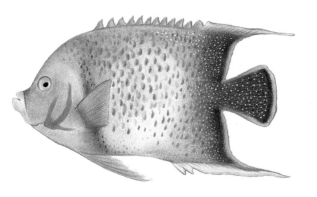

Royal angelfish
Pygoplites diacanthus

Elongated body, which is not very wide; pointed snout hollowed at the back; small terminal mouth; rounded caudal fin. Orange in color with vertical white and blue stripes; yellow caudal fin, orange and blue anal fin. Lives along outer slope of reef from 3 to 165 feet (1 to 50 meters). Grows to 10 inches (25 centimeters).

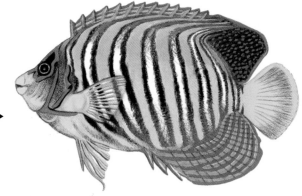

Bicolor cherub or oriole angelfish
Centropyge bicolor

Oval, compressed, bicolor body. The front is yellow with a blue spot over the eyes; the back is blue with a yellow caudal fin. Prefers coralline sea beds and sheltered environments, such as lagoons, but never ventures far from shelter. Grows up to 6 inches (15 centimeters).

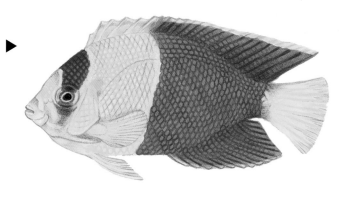

Two-spined angelfish
Centropyge bispinosus

Oval, compressed body; rounded head; terminal mouth; two rays at base of operculum. Coloration is bluish and orange on belly, with black, more or less visible, vertical striations on flanks. Generally lives on external reefs from 15 to 150 feet (5 to 45 meters). Measures up to 4 inches (10 centimeters).

Multibarred angelfish
Centropyge multifasciatus

Small, oval, compressed body; rounded head; short snout. Whitish coloration with more or less visible black and yellow vertical streaks on flanks; yellow ventral and anal fins. Generally lives on outer reefs, near grottos, from 23 to 230 feet (7 to 70 meters). Grows to over 4 inches (11 centimeters).

POMACENTRIDAE FAMILY

Sergeant major
Abdudefduf vaigensis

Oval body; convex snout; small terminal mouth with conical teeth and incisors. Common in large numbers in various habitats: lagoons, flat sea beds, reef slopes. Lives in schools and feeds on zooplankton, small invertebrates, and sea-floor algae. Grows up to 8 inches (20 centimeters).

Clown anemonefish
Amphiprion percula

Oval, slightly compressed body; rounded snout. Orange in color with three vertical, black-edged white bands on flanks. Lives in lagoons and along the reef at depths of up to 50 feet (15 meters); associates with *Stichodactyla* and *Heteractis* anemones. Grows to 4 inches (11 centimeters).

Dusky anemonefish
Amphiprion melanopus

Oval, somewhat compressed; rounded snout. Coloration is orange in the front and black in the rear of the body; opercula marked with a white band; black ventral and anal fins. Lives in lagoons and along reefs to 60 feet (18 meters); associates with *Entacmaea* anemones. Measures up to 5 inches (12 centimeters).

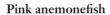

Pink anemonefish
Amphiprion perideraion

Oval, somewhat compressed body; rounded snout. Pinkish coloration with a white band behind the eyes. Lives in lagoons and along reefs to 100 feet (30 meters); associates with *Heteractis* anemones. Grows to 4 inches (10 centimeters).

Clark's anemonefish
Amphiprion clarkii

Oval, slightly compressed body; rounded snout. Dark in color with three white bands on flanks and a yellow spot on snout throat. Lives in lagoons and along reefs at depths of up to 200 feet (60 meters); associates with various species of anemones. Grows up to 5 inches (13 centimeters).

Spinecheek anemonefish
Premnas biaculeatus

Oval, slightly compressed body; small head; very short snout; dorsal fin has slight notch between spiny and soft rays; large spine under the eye. Males are bright red with three white, equidistant bands; females are less bright, sometimes almost black. Usually associates with *Entacentimetresaea quadricolour* anemone. Males grow 2 to 3 inches (5 to 8 centimeters) in length; females can grow two to three times larger.

Blue devil
Chrysiptera cynea

Oval body; distinct spiny rays on dorsal; caudal fin has rounded edges. Coloration varies according to sex: males are blue with a yellow tail, females are blue with a black spot on back portion of dorsal fin. Both have a black stripe crossing the snout and eye. Prefers lagoons and sheltered reefs. Measures up to 3 inches (8 centimeters).

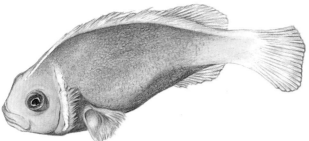

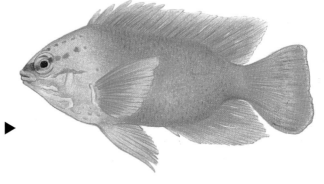

White-belly damselfish
Amblyglyphidon leucogaster

Oval, tall, and compressed body; clearly forked tail; pointed snout; terminal mouth; extremities of ventral fins are filamentous. Coloration is blue-green on the back, whitish on belly; black tip on odd fins. Lives alone or in small groups along reefs between 6 and 100 feet (2 and 34 meters). Measures up to 5 inches (13 centimeters).

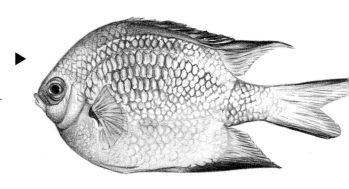

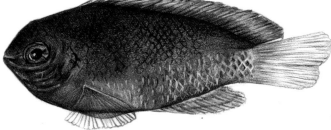

Three-spot dascyllus
Dascyllus trimaculatus

Rounded, tall, compressed body. Coloration is black with a white spot on flanks; young specimens also have a white spot on front. Young often live among sea anemones; adults live close to corals at depths varying between 3 and 165 feet (1 and 50 meters). Measures up to 5.5 inches (14 centimeters).

Bigscaled scalyfin
Parma oligolepis

Compressed, oval body of average height; forked tail; pointed head; somewhat oversize mouth. Coloration is dark. Lives mainly on rocky sea beds from 6 to 65 feet (2 to 20 meters). Grows to over 8 inches (21 centimeters).

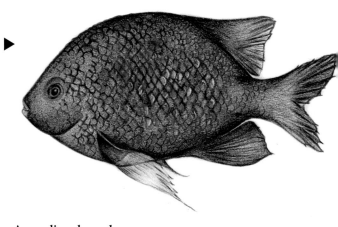

Australian damsel
Pomacentrus australis

Compressed oval body; slightly forked tail; pointed head; somewhat oversized mouth. Bluish coloration on back, brighter toward belly. Lives mainly near coral colonies or rock heaps on sandy sea beds from 15 to 115 feet (5 to 35 meters). Measures up to 3 inches (8 centimeters).

Yellow-spotted chromis
Chromis flavomaculata

Oval, tall, compressed body; clearly forked tail; blunt snout; mouth turns upward. Light coloration; black edge on dorsal fin; dark spot at base of pectoral fins; black-and-white anal fin; yellow caudal fin. Lives in schools above corals between 20 and 130 feet (6 and 40 meters). Grows up to 6.5 inches (16 centimeters).

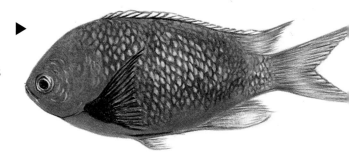

LABRIDAE FAMILY

Diana's hogfish
Bodianus diana

Elongated, compressed body; pointed snout; tail has a more or less straight margin. Reddish coloration, especially on the head; body is overspread with yellow; some lighter spots along the back. Adults live alone along the outer reef between 15 and 80 feet (5 and 25 meters). Measures up to 10 inches (25 centimeters).

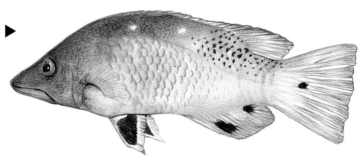

Harlequin tuskfish
Choerodon fasciatus

High, oval, somewhat compressed body; rounded snout; thick, canine, partially exposed teeth. Coloration marked by large, vertical, alternating bands in white and orange. Feeds on mollusks and crustaceans. Territorial and solitary; lives around 50 to 65 feet (15 to 20 meters). Measures up to 10 inches (25 centimeters).

Yellowtail wrasse
Anampses meleagrides

Oval, tapered body; pointed snout; terminal mouth; robust and prominent canines in both jaws. Females are blackish with white spots and yellow tail; males are dark with bluish stripes. Lives among corals and in sandy areas between 15 and 200 feet (5 and 60 meters). Grows to 9 inches (22 centimeters).

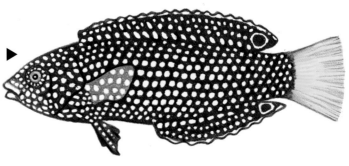

Clown wrasse
Coris aygula

Tapered, compressed body; pointed snout on young individuals and females; concave with a frontal protuberance in adult males. Young specimens are whitish in color with orange ocellar spots; females are whitish with fins edged in black; males are greenish blue with a vertical white band. Solitary and lives near corals and in sandy areas to 100 feet (30 meters). Measures up to 28 inches (70 centimeters).

Checkerboard wrasse
Halichoeres hortulanus

Tapered body, compressed at the back; pointed snout. Greenish in color with white spots edged in black longitudinally on flanks; dorsal fin preceded by a yellow-and-black spot. Lives at around 100 feet (30 meters) on sandy sea floors, where it burrows to hide or hunt for small invertebrates. Measures up to 11 inches (27 centimeters).

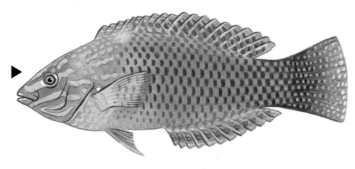

Dusky wrasse
Halichoeres marginatus

Tapered body of medium height, compressed toward the rear; rounded snout. Greenish head; lateral dark stripes and bluish band on tail. Lives in lagoons and on reefs richest in coral to 100 feet (30 meters). Grows to 11 inches (27 centimeters).

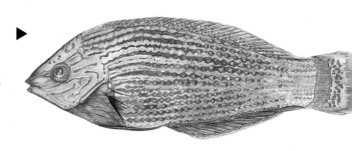

Bird wrasse
Gomphosus varius

Elongated, tapered body; pointed head; very long, tubular snout. Males are dark blue and greenish; the back portion of females is gray with dark spots on the scales. Lives in lagoons or coral-filled reefs to 100 feet (30 meters). Grows to over 10 inches (26 centimeters).

Bicolor cleaner wrasse
Labroides bicolor

Tapered body, compressed toward the rear; elongated snout; small, terminal mouth. Coloration is blue in front with a black band in the center; rear is yellow. Belongs to the cleaner wrasse group, but is not territorial; moves from one point to another in the reef at a depth of 100 feet (30 meters). Grows to almost 5 inches (12 centimeters).

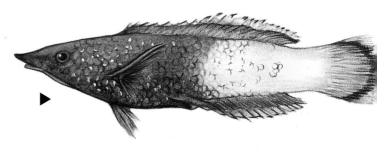

Cleaner wrasse
Labroides dimidiatus

Tapered body, compressed at the back; elongated snout; small terminal mouth. Light blue in color with a black band that gradually widens from mouth to caudal fin. Territorial; lives at depths of 130 to 150 feet (40 to 45 meters); noted for attracting fish, which it cleans of parasites and detritus. Measures up to 4 inches (10 centimeters).

SCARIDAE FAMILY

Bicolor parrotfish
Cetoscarus bicolor

Somewhat tapered and oval body; pointed snout; crescent-shaped caudal fin with pointed lobes. Females are brownish with a thick series of dark spots on lower part of the body; males have bluish heads with tiny fuchsia spots; dorsal region and flanks are green with scales edged in fuchsia. Lives in pairs. Grows up to 31.5 inches (80 centimeters).

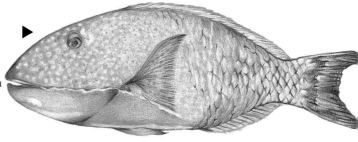

Swarthy parrotfish
Scarus niger

Tapered body; round snout; tail somewhat crescent-shaped with pointed lobes. Coloration is typically swarthy (brownish red in the females) with a white spot on the operculum. Usually lives alone in lagoons and channels rich in coral to a depth of 50 feet (15 meters). Grows to 14 inches (35 centimeters).

Flame parrotfish
Scarus ghobban

Tapered body; rounded snout; lips cover part of the pink or green dental plates. Greenish in color with pink-edged scales. Lives in lagoons and along the outer reef to 80 feet (25 meters). Grows up to 16 inches (40 centimeters).

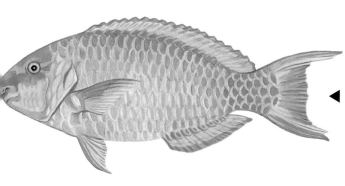

Bullethead parrotfish
Scarus sordidus

Body shape typical of parrotfish; dental plates clearly visible. Young have horizontal stripes and become brown in color as they mature; adult males are green with salmon-edged scales and bright orange cheeks that fade into yellow on the opercula; very peculiar green teeth; females have red mouths. Measures from 16 to 20 inches (40 to 50 centimeters).

SPHYRAENIDAE FAMILY

Blackfin barracuda
Sphyraena genie

Characteristically elongated body; pointed head; wide mouth with strong, sharp teeth; two very distinct dorsal fins; caudal fin is sickle-shaped with pointed lobes. Silvery in color with dark fins and slightly curved brown bands along flanks. Lives in schools in areas swept by currents, at 50 to 65 feet (15 to 20 meters). Grows up to 4.5 feet (1.7 meters).

Pickhandle barracuda
Sphyraena jello

Characteristically elongated body; pointed head; wide mouth with strong, sharp teeth; two clearly distinct dorsal fins; caudal fin is bilobed. Coloration is silvery with light fins and brown vertical spots along flanks; caudal fin is yellowish. Lives in schools in areas swept by currents, at 50 to 65 feet (15 to 20 meters). Measures up to 4 feet (1.5 meters).

PINGUIPEDIDAE FAMILY

Speckled sandperch
Parapercis hexophthalma

Elongated body, somewhat compressed; terminal mouth with strong, canine-shaped teeth. Light greenish brown in color on back and white on belly, with swarthy spots; caudal fin is black. Lives on sandy sea beds at 65 to 80 feet (20 to 25 meters). Measures over 10 inches (26 centimeters).

TRYPTERYGIDAE FAMILY

Striped triplefin
Helcogramma striata

Small, moderately elongated body; rounded snout; three dorsal fins. Coloration is reddish with three thin, bright streaks on flanks. Lives on coral sea beds, camouflaged among sponges, corals, and gorgonians at 23 to 33 feet (7 to 10 meters). Measures up to 1.5 inches (4 centimeters).

BLENNIDAE FAMILY

Yellowtail poison fangblenny
Meiacanthus atrodorsalis

Tapered body, compressed toward the rear; long, low dorsal fin; blunt snout; mouth equipped with sharp, hollow teeth connected to venomous glands. Coloration is grayish blue in front and yellow in the rear. Lives in lagoons and on reefs to a depth of 100 feet (30 meters). Measures up to 4 inches (11 centimeters).

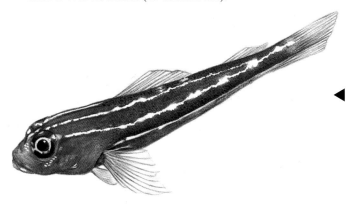

Lined fangblenny
Meiacanthus lineatus

Tapered body, compressed toward the rear; long, low dorsal fin; blunt snout; mouth equipped with sharp, hollow teeth connected to venomous glands. Coloration features black and yellow longitudinal streaks; white belly; yellow tail. Lives on reefs to a depth of 65 to 80 feet (20 to 25 meters). Measures up to 3.7 inches (9.5 centimeters).

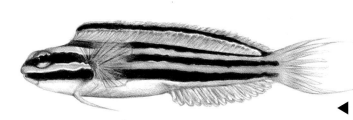

Filamentous blenny
Cirripectes filamentosus

Stocky body with a large and blunt head; long dorsal fin with elongated first ray; small tentacles on snout and near eyes; wide mouth equipped with numerous teeth in comblike formation. Coloration is brownish with orange streaks on snout and front part of the trunk. Lives on rocky and coral sea beds to a depth of 65 feet (20 meters). Measures up to 3.5 inches (9 centimeters).

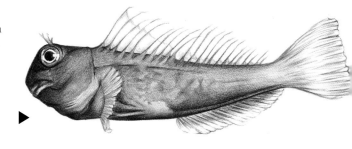

Bicolor blenny
Ecsenius bicolor

Elongated and compressed body; head features an almost vertical front profile; well-developed dorsal fin; slightly rounded caudal fin. Coloration is bluish in front and yellow toward the rear. A brown variety with uniform color exists. Lives in lagoons on sea beds with a combination of rock and coral to a depth of 80 feet (25 meters). Measures up to 4 inches (10 centimeters).

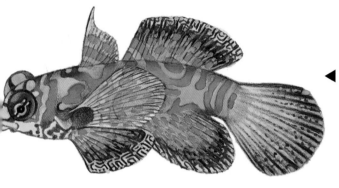

CALLIONYMIDAE FAMILY

Mandarin fish
Synchiropus splendidus

Small, slightly sunken body; no scales; large head; two dorsal fins. Brightly colored but extremely mimetic—becomes completely invisible to its predators. Lives on muddy sea floors among corals and detritus to depths of 60 feet (18 meters). Measures up to 2.3 inches (6 centimeters).

GOBIIDAE FAMILY

Steinitz's prawn goby
Amblyeleotris steinitzi

Small, elongated body; short, truncated snout; large lips. Coloration is light with dark diagonal bands on flanks; dorsal fin is bluish with orange spots. Lives on sandy sea beds at 15 to 100 feet (5 to 30 meters), sharing its den with a commensal shrimp. Grows to 3 inches (8 centimeters).

Bluestriped goby
Valenciennea striata

Elongated body, compressed at the back, flattened ventrally; ventral fins are close but not fused. Front of body is golden in color, with a blue stripe from mouth to pectoral fin; rest of the body is whitish with diagonal red stripes on lower part of flanks and horizontal stripes on fins. Lives in pairs in lagoons and along outer reefs at depths of from 3 to 65 feet (1 to 20 meters); digs dens in coralline and sandy sea beds. Measures up to 7 inches (18 centimeters).

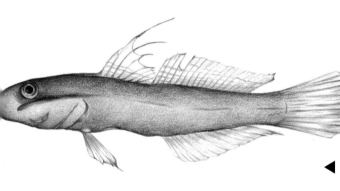

Crab-eye goby
Signigobius biocellatus

Massive body on a small fish; large, blunt head; two quite wide dorsal fins; well-developed anal fin. Coloration is brownish; large ocellate spots on dorsal fins serve to scare off aggressors; ventral and anal fins are dark with blue spots. Lives in pairs in dens on sandy sea beds to a depth of 100 feet (30 meters). Grows up to 2.5 inches (6.5 centimeters).

Citron goby
Gobiodon citrinus

Massive subcylindric head, taller toward the front; the two dorsals are very close. Coloration is intense yellow with blue streaks behind the opercula. Lives among acropora branches at 65 to 80 feet (20 to 25 meters). Produces a bitter toxic mucus when touched. Grows to 2.6 inches (6.6 centimeters).

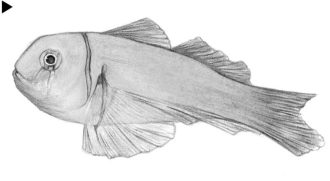

ACANTHURIDAE FAMILY

Sailfin tang
Zebrasoma veliferum

Compressed, disc-shaped body; well-developed dorsal fin and anal fins; pointed snout; small, terminal mouth. Coloration features white and brown alternating stripes with a yellow tail. Lives in lagoons and along reef to a depth of 100 feet (30 meters). Grows to 16 inches (40 centimeters).

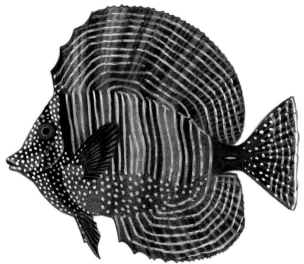

Palette surgeonfish
Paracanthurus hepatus

Oval, tapered, compressed body. Coloration is blue with black bands on flanks; pectoral fins are edged in yellow; caudal fin is yellow. Lives in small schools in areas dominated by currents and rich in plankton at 6 to 130 feet (2 to 40 meters). Measures over 12 inches (31 centimeters).

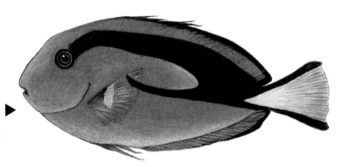

Whitecheek surgeonfish
Acanthurus nigricans

Oval, tall, compressed body; falciform (crescent-shaped) caudal fin. Brownish coloration with yellow bands on base of dorsal fin, anal fin, and spines; eyes and mouth lined with white; white caudal fin. Lives in lagoons and in exposed areas of the reef to a depth of 200 to 230 feet (60 to 70 meters). Measures over 8 inches (21 centimeters).

Brown surgeonfish
Acanthurus nigrofuscus

Oval body; small mouth with thick lips; crescent-shaped caudal fin. Light brown in color with lavender tones, especially on fins; body overspread with small orange spots. Feeds on filamentous algae. Grows to over 8 inches (21 centimeters).

Bluestriped surgeonfish
Acanthurus lineatus

Elongated, oval, compressed body; rounded snout; sickle-shaped pectoral fins; crescent-shaped caudal fin with very elongated lobes; large spine on caudal peduncle. Coloration features 8 to 10 longitudinal yellow and blue stripes on flanks; light-colored belly; yellow ventral fins tipped with black on the front margin. Territorial and aggressive; most common on reefs exposed to the waves. Grows up to 15 inches (38 centimeters).

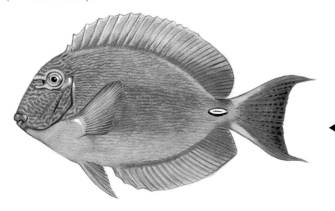

Striped-eye surgeonfish
Acanthurus dussumieri

Elongated, oval, compressed body; snout has a blunt upper profile; sickle-shaped caudal fin with pointed lobes. Light in color with an orange band over the eyes; black stripe at edge of opercula; yellowish fins; caudal fin edged in blue. Lives along the outer reef at 33 to 425 feet (10 to 130 meters). Grows to almost 22 inches (54 centimeters).

Orangespined unicornfish
Naso lituratus

Oval, compressed body, wide to the front; robust head with a dorsal profile that forms about a 45° angle; pointed snout; small mouth armed with incisors with rounded tips; two bony plaques on peduncle sides, each of which has a sharp curved spine pointed forward; semicrescent-shaped caudal fin with pointed lobes and long, filamentous rays. Yellowish brown in color; orange caudal peduncle; light yellow spot between the eyes; dorsal fin is orange-yellow, black at the base, with a white edge. Grows to 18 inches (45 centimeters).

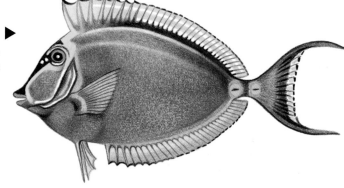

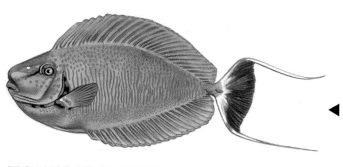

SIGANIDAE FAMILY

Bignosed unicornfish
Naso vlammingi

Robust, tapered body, somewhat oval; mouth has almost vertical front profile; very long, threadlike lobes on caudal fin. During the day it tends to form schools, feeding on plankton in the column of water over the reef. Can change color rapidly. Grows to 28 inches (70 centimeters).

Foxface rabbitfish
Siganus vulpinus

Oval, slightly rounded body; pointed snout with concave profile; small, terminal mouth has numerous incisor-shaped teeth; poisonous spiny rays on fins. Yellow in color; white head with dark bands extending to throat. Lives in pairs in coral-rich waters at around 100 feet (30 meters). Grows to over 9 inches (24 centimeters).

Coral rabbitfish
Siganus corallinus

Oval, somewhat rounded body; slightly pointed snout; small terminal mouth equipped with numerous incisor-shaped teeth; spiny rays on fins are venomous. Coloration is yellow, densely covered by blue spots. Lives in pairs in lagoons and areas rich in coral from 80 to 100 feet (25 to 30 meters). Grows to 11 inches (28 centimeters).

BALISTIDAE FAMILY

Redtooth triggerfish
Odonus niger

Suboval body; pointed head; terminal mouth with overdeveloped lower jaw; peculiar red, canine-shaped teeth. Bluish black body; greenish head with bluish stripes that run from the mouth; semicrescent-shaped caudal fin with very large, long lobes. Tends to gather in small groups. Measures 20 inches (50 centimeters).

Yellowmargin triggerfish
Pseudobalistes flavimarginatus

Oval, compressed, wide body; robust mouth with two rows of white teeth on upper jaw and one on lower jaw. Basic color is rather light; front portion between snout and base of pectoral fins light yellow; flanks distinguished by black spots; yellowish edges on dorsal, anal, and caudal fins. Grows to 24 inches (60 centimeters).

Boomerang triggerfish
Sufflamen bursa

Tapered, subquadrangular body; pointed head with a triangular, concave lower profile. Light brown in color with a dark band from operculum to eyes; whitish front ventral portion. Lives in coral-rich, sheltered areas between 10 and 295 feet (3 and 90 meters). Grows to over 10 inches (24 centimeters).

Orange-striped triggerfish
Balistapus undulatus

Squat, subquadrangular, compressed body; large head; mouth has strong, scalpel-shaped teeth; caudal peduncle has spiny scales. Greenish brown in color with orange stripes that cover its entire body. Lives in coral-rich areas to 165 feet (50 meters). Measures up to 12 inches (30 centimeters).

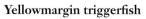
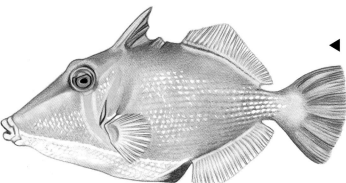
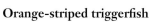

Halfmoon Picassofish
Rhinecanthus lunula

Subquadrangular, tapered, compressed body; head profile is almost triangular. Coloration is light with orange or brownish streaks along flanks; orange spot on the caudal peduncle. Lives along the outer slopes of reefs between 33 and 130 feet (10 and 40 meters). Measures up to 11 inches (28 centimeters).

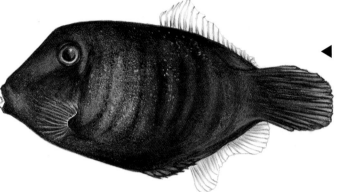

MONACANTHIDAE FAMILY

Broom filefish
Amanses scopas

Compressed, lozenge-shaped body; pointed snout; first dorsal consists of a single, sturdy spiny ray; scales covered by thin, filamentous structures. Males have numerous long spines on the rear of their flanks. Coloration is brown with dark vertical streaks. Lives on sea beds with a combination of sand and coral from 10 to 60 feet (3 to 18 meters). Measures over 6 inches (16 centimeters).

Harlequin filefish
Oxymonacanthus longirostris

Long, tapered body; clearly elongated snout; small, upturned mouth; first dorsal fin, reduced to a single spiny ray, is above the eyes. Bluish green in color with yellow stripes and a black spot on lower lobe of caudal fin. Lives at about 100 feet (30 meters) among acropora corals, on which it feeds. Grows to almost 5 inches (12 centimeters) in length.

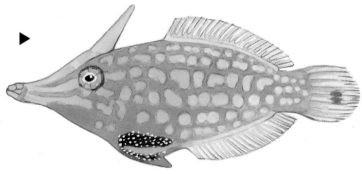

OSTRACIIDAE FAMILY

Spotted trunkfish
Ostracion meleagris

Stocky body composed of polygonal plates welded together, from which the mouth and the fin fissures open. Coloration is bluish with yellow spots scattered on the body. Lives in lagoons and along the outer reef to 100 feet (30 meters). Grows to over 6 inches (16 centimeters).

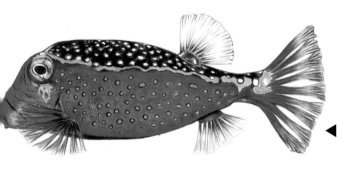

TETRAODONTIDAE FAMILY

Map puffer
Arothron mappa

Subcylindrical body; slightly pointed snout. Light coloration with dark spots that are larger on the back; eyes surrounded by dense rays of stripes. Solitary and lives in lagoons and along the outer slopes of reef to 100 feet (30 meters), keeping close to the crevices. Grows to 26 inches (65 centimeters).

I would like to thank those who helped me in creating this guide, beginning with Carlo Chiaraluce of Garuda Airlines, Daniela di Monaco of Qantas Airlines, and Ms. Nicolosi of Ansett Australia Airlines. Many people on the staff of Queensland Tourism and Travel Corporation and of the Australian Tourist Commission also provided vital assistance. At sea, the experience and knowledge of Mike Ball, Ron Steven, and Michael Goodings of Mike Ball Diving Expeditions proved to be invaluable. I would also like to thank the crew of the Rum Runner *motor sailer. Finally, my heartfelt thanks to Federica Calderini, my trusted traveling and diving companion, who handled all the logistical organization herself and shared all my difficulties in completing the work.*

ROBERTO RINALDI

Above:
Not everything is gigantic on the Australian sea beds: under a macro-photography lens, coral blocks and gorgonians reveal a microcosm rich in invertebrates, such as this tiny mimetic crab.

Front cover:
Enormous sea fans grow on the floor of Midnite Reef.